Pipeline Accident Report

**Natural Gas Pipeline Rupture and Fire
Near Carlsbad, New Mexico
August 19, 2000**

NTSB/PAR-03/01
PB2003-916501
Notation 7310B
Adopted February 11, 2003

National Transportation Safety Board
490 L'Enfant Plaza, S.W.
Washington, D.C. 20594

National Transportation Safety Board. 2003. *Natural Gas Pipeline Rupture and Fire Near Carlsbad, New Mexico, August 19, 2000.* Pipeline Accident Report NTSB/PAR-03/01. Washington, D.C.

Abstract: At 5:26 a.m., mountain daylight time, on Saturday, August 19, 2000, a 30-inch-diameter natural gas transmission pipeline operated by El Paso Natural Gas Company ruptured adjacent to the Pecos River near Carlsbad, New Mexico. The released gas ignited and burned for 55 minutes. Twelve persons who were camping under a concrete-decked steel bridge that supported the pipeline across the river were killed and their three vehicles destroyed. Two nearby steel suspension bridges for gas pipelines crossing the river were extensively damaged. According to El Paso Natural Gas Company, property and other damages or losses totaled $998,296.

The major safety issues identified in this investigation are the design and construction of the pipeline, the adequacy of El Paso Natural Gas Company's internal corrosion control program, the adequacy of Federal safety regulations for natural gas pipelines, and the adequacy of Federal oversight of the pipeline operator.

As a result of its investigation of this accident, the National Transportation Safety Board makes safety recommendations to the Research and Special Programs Administration and NACE International.

Contents

Executive Summary v

Factual Information 1
   Accident Synopsis 1
   Accident Narrative 1
   Emergency Response 7
   Pipeline Operations After the Rupture 10
   Postaccident On-Site Inspection 10
   Injuries 11
   Damages 12
   Toxicological Information 12
   Tests and Research 13
      Metallurgical Examination 13
      Corrosion Products 15
   Pipeline 1103 16
      Pipeline Features 16
      Gas Suppliers 17
      Pigging Operations 18
      Tests and Inspections 21
   EPNG's Internal Corrosion Program 21
      Internal Corrosion Control Procedures 23
      Internal Audit Program 25
   Regulatory Oversight 26
      Federal Safety Standards 26
      Preaccident Federal Inspections of EPNG 28
      Federal Safety Standards and Enforcement—Maps and Records 29
   Postaccident Actions 30
      Pipeline Reconstruction 30
      Pipeline Integrity Management 31
      Federal Response 31
   Pipeline Integrity Management—Federal Regulations 33
   NACE Standards 35
   ASME Code for Gas Piping (B31.8) 35
   Guide for Gas Transmission and Distribution Piping Systems 36
   Other Information 36
      Previous EPNG Internal Corrosion Accident 36
      Emergency Training and Simulations 37

Analysis 38
   Exclusions 38
   Emergency Response 39
   Internal Corrosion in Steel Gas Pipelines 39
   Internal Corrosion in Line 1103 40
   Physical Features of Line 1103 41
   EPNG Internal Corrosion Control Program 43

Federal Safety Regulations 46
Federal Oversight of the Pipeline Operator 46
Industry Standards 48

Conclusions 49
Findings 49
Probable Cause 50

Recommendations 51

Appendixes
A: Investigation 53
B: Summary of Office of Pipeline Safety Corrective Action Order 54
C: Research and Special Programs Administration Advisory Bulletin 56

Executive Summary

At 5:26 a.m., mountain daylight time, on Saturday, August 19, 2000, a 30-inch-diameter natural gas transmission pipeline operated by El Paso Natural Gas Company ruptured adjacent to the Pecos River near Carlsbad, New Mexico. The released gas ignited and burned for 55 minutes. Twelve persons who were camping under a concrete-decked steel bridge that supported the pipeline across the river were killed and their three vehicles destroyed. Two nearby steel suspension bridges for gas pipelines crossing the river were extensively damaged. According to El Paso Natural Gas Company, property and other damages or losses totaled $998,296.

The National Transportation Safety Board determines that the probable cause of the August 19, 2000, natural gas pipeline rupture and subsequent fire near Carlsbad, New Mexico, was a significant reduction in pipe wall thickness due to severe internal corrosion. The severe corrosion had occurred because El Paso Natural Gas Company's corrosion control program failed to prevent, detect, or control internal corrosion within the company's pipeline. Contributing to the accident were ineffective Federal preaccident inspections of El Paso Natural Gas Company that did not identify deficiencies in the company's internal corrosion control program.

The major safety issues identified in this investigation are as follows:

- The design and construction of the pipeline,
- The adequacy of El Paso Natural Gas Company's internal corrosion control program,
- The adequacy of Federal safety regulations for natural gas pipelines, and
- The adequacy of Federal oversight of the pipeline operator.

As a result of its investigation of this accident, the National Transportation Safety Board makes safety recommendations to the Research and Special Programs Administration and NACE International.

Factual Information

Accident Synopsis

At 5:26 a.m., mountain daylight time, on Saturday, August 19, 2000, a 30-inch-diameter natural gas transmission pipeline operated by El Paso Natural Gas Company (EPNG) ruptured adjacent to the Pecos River near Carlsbad, New Mexico. The released gas ignited and burned for 55 minutes. Twelve persons who were camping under a concrete-decked steel bridge that supported the pipeline across the river were killed and their three vehicles destroyed. Two nearby steel suspension bridges for gas pipelines crossing the river were extensively damaged. According to EPNG, property and other damages or losses totaled $998,296.

Accident Narrative

The EPNG pipeline system (figure 1) transported gas west from Texas and New Mexico to Arizona and California. A portion of the pipeline system crossed the Pecos River about 4 1/2 miles north of the Texas-New Mexico State line and 30 miles south of Carlsbad, New Mexico. (See figure 2.) About 1 mile west of the river crossing was the Pecos River compressor station, which received gas from four natural gas transmission pipelines—26-inch-diameter line 1100, 30-inch-diameter line 1103, 30-inch-diameter line 1110, and 16-inch-diameter line 3191. Three of these lines (1100, 1103, and 1110) ran parallel to Whitethorn Road (also known as Pipeline Road) from the Pecos River to the Pecos River compressor station. Lines 1103 and 1110 were supported at the river crossing by a one-lane concrete-decked steel service bridge that was not open to the public. (See figure 3.) (This bridge, which had been built by EPNG in 1950, also supported a water pipeline and a gas gathering pipeline. EPNG, which was at the time of the accident a subsidiary of El Paso Energy, owned and operated the water pipeline but not the gas gathering pipeline.) Line 1100 was supported across the river on a pipeline suspension bridge approximately 70 feet northeast of the service bridge. Another EPNG pipeline, 16-inch-diameter line 1000, was supported by a separate suspension bridge in this area, but this line had been removed from service and was filled with nitrogen at the time of the accident. The fourth pipeline, line 3191, ran from EPNG's South Carlsbad compressor station to the Pecos River compressor station.

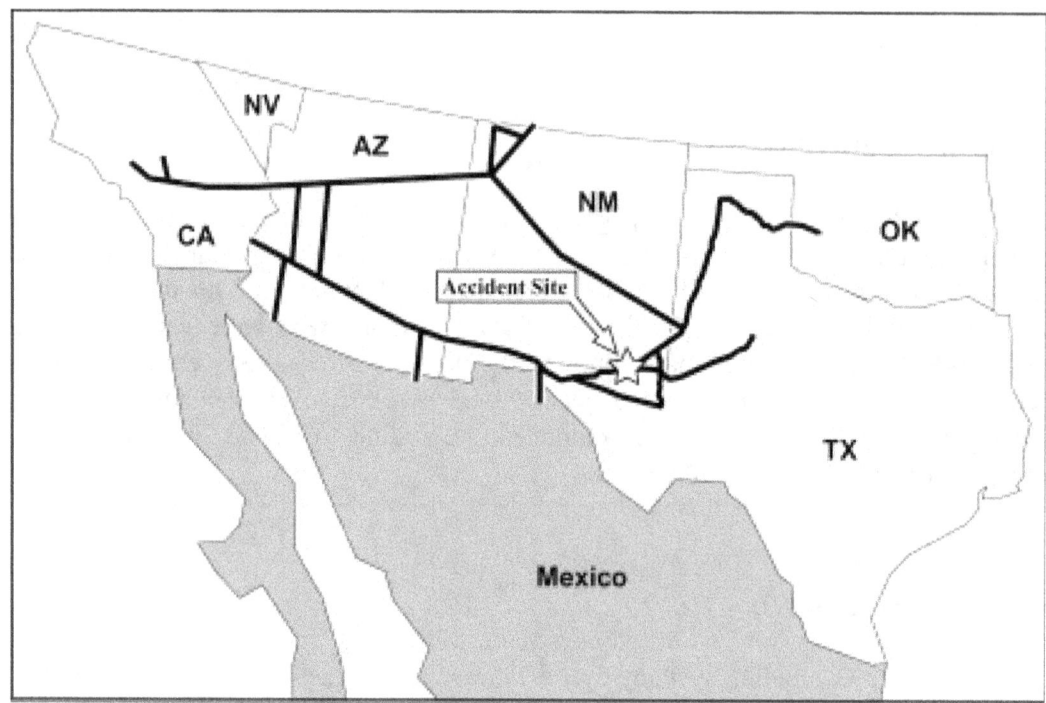

Figure 1. El Paso Natural Gas system.

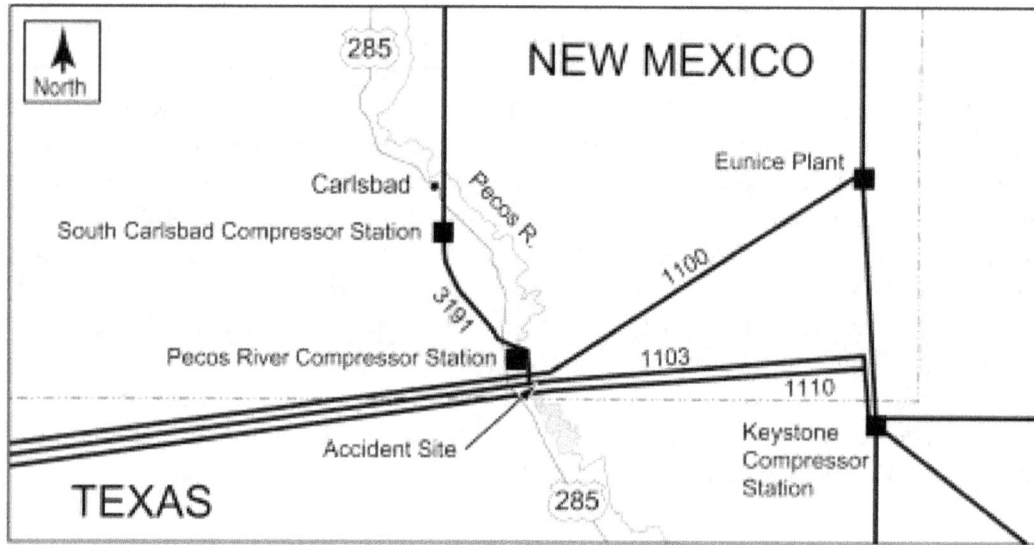

Figure 2. Accident area.

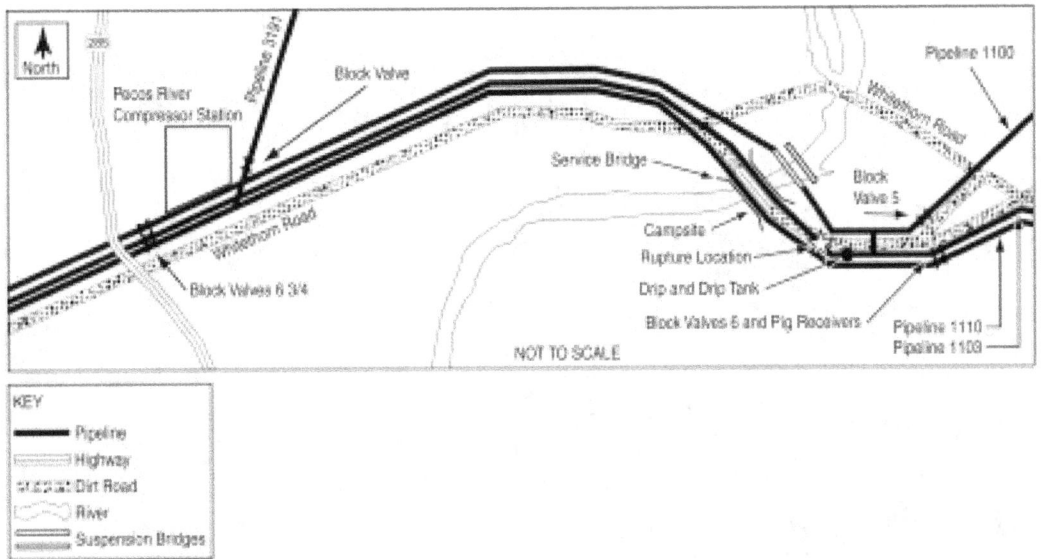

Figure 3. Accident site.

At the time of the accident, 12 members of an extended family were camping on the east bank of the Pecos River near the service bridge.[1] (See figure 4.) A locked wire rope and a "Private Right of Way—No Trespassing" sign at each entrance to the bridge restricted access to the bridge above the campsite. Two "Caution—High Pressure Gas Line" signs were posted near the east entrance to the service bridge. Also, a sign reading as follows:

> Warning - No Trespassing - This road and right of way is private property and is not for public use. This pipeline carries natural gas under high pressure and is dangerous. All persons are warned of the danger to person and property. KEEP OFF

had been posted alongside the right-of-way road (near the intersection with the county road) leading past the block valves and pig receivers to the service bridge on the east side of the river. The pipeline system was operated from EPNG's gas control center in El Paso, Texas, as a north system and a south system. The gas control center was equipped with three supervisory control and data acquisition (SCADA)[2] system work consoles, each of which was capable of displaying data for both pipeline systems.

On the morning of August 19, 2000, three EPNG employees, a coordinator of pipeline control (who was in charge of the shift) and two gas controllers, were nearing the

---

[1] At the time of the accident, a private landowner owned the accident site. After the accident, EPNG purchased this property and installed fencing to restrict access to the area.

[2] Pipeline controllers use a computer-based SCADA system to remotely monitor and control movement of gas through pipelines. The system makes it possible to monitor operating parameters critical to pipeline operations, such as flow rates, pressures, equipment status, control valve positions, and alarms indicating abnormal conditions.

Figure 4. Aerial view of accident site looking east.

end of their 12-hour shifts at the gas control center. One of the controllers was operating the north system and the other the south, while the coordinator assisted the two controllers and performed administrative oversight and served as a backup controller when needed. The two controllers were working at separate SCADA terminals to monitor and control pipeline operations. The employees said they had noted no unusual operating conditions during their shift, and no unusual conditions had been noted during the previous 12-hour shift.

The south system controller, at 5:26 a.m.,[3] received SCADA rate-of-change[4] alarms for the speed of compressor unit No. 3 at the Pecos River compressor station.[5] Less than a minute later, compressor unit No. 1 at the station shut down, quickly followed by the automatic closing and opening of station valves, as appropriate, to isolate the compressor station from the pipeline. Emergency lubricating oil pumps were also automatically activated at the station. A few seconds later, additional alarms from the station displayed on the controller's monitor, including a rate-of-change alarm for falling

---

[3] Times in this section are based on SCADA event data recorder records, controller logs, and personnel statements and interviews.

[4] *Rate-of-change* alarms indicate that a measured variable, such as compressor speed or compressor suction pressure, is increasing or decreasing at a rate exceeding what would be expected under normal operating conditions.

[5] The unattended Pecos River compressor station had three turbine compressors.

suction (inlet) pressure at the station. (Unknown to the controller at the time, pressure on the inlet side of the station dropped because pipeline 1103 had ruptured near the river crossing.) Noting the alarms, the south controller began to request SCADA data for the Pecos River compressor station instead of waiting for the data to appear from the automatic data scans, which occurred at 4-minute intervals.[6]

At about this time, the transmission of SCADA data between the gas control center and the Pecos River compressor station was briefly interrupted. According to the south controller, he was immediately alerted to the data interruption by the display of inverse video on his SCADA monitor. Inverse video indicated that a proper reply to a request for data from the SCADA system had not been received and that the displayed data were not being updated. Although not recorded in the SCADA system event log, this interruption lasted about 30 seconds.

At approximately 5:30 a.m., the controller telephoned the Pecos River district station lead operations specialist[7] at home and asked him to send people to the Pecos River compressor station. The south controller later stated:

> I noted that we did have a low suction pressure, and generally when our plants go down, the suction pressure goes up instead of down. I told [the station lead operations specialist], 'We need to get somebody out there right away because I think we have a problem.'

The station lead operations specialist called two operations specialists that he supervised and who were on duty and told them to go to the Pecos River compressor station.

About the same time the station lead operations specialist was making this call, an EPNG operations specialist from the Carlsbad complex, who was at his home south of the city of Carlsbad, noticed a glow in the sky to the south. (See figure 5.) He said he immediately suspected that an EPNG pipeline may be involved. He called the gas control center and asked if its personnel had noticed any sudden pressure changes at the Pecos River compressor station. He told center personnel of the glow in the sky and said that he suspected a rupture. The north controller informed him that EPNG had lost a compressor at the Pecos River compressor station.

The operations specialist then telephoned his supervisor (the pipeline lead operations specialist), and informed him of the glow in the sky and of his call to the gas control center. He then told the pipeline lead operations specialist that he was on his way to the Pecos River compressor station.

---

[6] This SCADA system logged operational data and transferred it to the gas control center via modem.

[7] EPNG had two employees in the Pecos River district with the official title "lead operations specialist." One lead operations specialist supervised operations specialists responsible for operating and maintaining compressor and meter stations. Another lead operations specialist supervised operations specialists responsible for operating and maintaining pipelines. This report refers to the two employees, respectively, as the *station* lead operations specialist and the *pipeline* lead operations specialist.

Figure 5. Post-rupture fire. At lower left of fireball can be seen the 85-foot-tall support structures for the pipeline suspension bridges.

At 5:31 a.m., the gas control center in El Paso again experienced an interruption in SCADA data transmission from the Pecos River compressor station, which prevented the controller's receiving any additional information from the station. The interruption occurred when the emergency shutdown system at the Pecos River compressor station activated, which caused a loss of power to the local SCADA computer and modem. The station was equipped with an uninterruptible power supply, but the station SCADA computer and modem were not connected to it.[8] SCADA communications with the Pecos River compressor station were restored at 9:04 a.m. on August 19.

At 5:35 a.m., the south controller again telephoned the station lead operations specialist at home and told him that he suspected a possible line blowout. At this time, the south controller did not know which pipeline was involved. The station lead operations specialist said that after looking out a window of his home in the direction of the Pecos River compressor station, he told the south controller that he could see a fire and that he was on his way to the Pecos River compressor station.

---

[8] The station was equipped with an uninterruptible power supply to maintain AC power to the station computer and hazardous gas and fire detection equipment. A 24-volt DC backup system maintained power to oil pumps, nozzle cooling water equipment, and other emergency equipment in the event of a station power failure.

At 5:44 a.m., the south controller called the Keystone compressor station[9] and asked the operator to take down three compressor units. About a minute later, he called the Eunice plant[10] and made the same request.

At 5:50 a.m., the south controller called El Paso Field Services to make sure that personnel there would shut down all compressor units at the South Carlsbad compressor station.[11] The south controller's shift ended at 6:00 a.m., but he stayed at the gas control center until 8:00 a.m. to provide assistance as necessary. During this time, he notified the El Paso Energy public relations department in Houston, Texas.[12]

Emergency Response

Within 5 minutes of the rupture, at 5:31 a.m., the local 911 operator received numerous calls from residents reporting a fire and the sound of an explosion. An off-duty EPNG employee who lived near the site also called 911 and reported the fire. The gas control center was called by an off-duty operations specialist when he saw light in the sky from the fire, and he also called the pipeline lead operations specialist for the local section of the pipeline.

That pipeline lead operations specialist was the first to arrive at the accident site, at about 5:45 a.m. He said that while he was en route, he had spoken with the gas control center and the EPNG general dispatcher from his truck and had asked the control center to call managers for the Jal and Carlsbad complexes. He recalled that as he neared the Pecos River compressor station, the fire was so bright that he had trouble seeing the road.

He then went to the pipeline on the west side of the Pecos River compressor station and began closing valves that were downstream from the fire. As he closed block (shutoff) valve No. 6 3/4 on line 1100, the operations specialist who had telephoned him earlier arrived, and the two men closed block valves No. 6 3/4 on lines 1103 and 1110. They also closed the pig launcher valves on these pipelines.[13]

The pipeline lead operations specialist and the operations specialist then drove their trucks to the west side of the service bridge and viewed the fire across the river, but

---

[9] The Keystone compressor station, an attended station about 57 miles east and upstream of the Pecos River compressor station, supplied gas to the Pecos River compressor station through lines 1103 and 1110.

[10] The Eunice plant, an attended station about 53 miles northeast and upstream of the Pecos River River station, supplied gas to the Pecos River compressor station through line 1100.

[11] The South Carlsbad compressor station, an attended station about 25 miles north and upstream of the Pecos station, supplied gas to the Pecos River compressor station through line 3191.

[12] Notifying the public relations department, which was responsible for responding to inquiries regarding events involving the company, was part of EPNG's emergency response procedures.

[13] *Pig* refers to any of a variety of mechanical devices that can be introduced into a pipeline system either to clean the pipeline or, through use of various detection technologies, to identify possible pipeline defects. Pig launchers and pig receivers in lines 1100, 1103, and 1110 at the time of the accident were used only for cleaning pigs.

they could not determine which line had ruptured. The pipeline lead operations specialist said he then told the operations specialist to go around to the other side of the river and attempt to determine which line had failed.

The operations specialist said he drove across the river at the low-water crossing and viewed the scene, but because of the proximity of the lines to one another and the fire, he could not determine which line had ruptured. The operations specialist said that as he was returning to where he left the pipeline lead operations specialist, he thought he may have seen vehicles in the fire area just south of the bridge. He continued back across the river to assist the pipeline lead operations specialist and also told him about the possibility of vehicles in the fire area. The pipeline lead operations specialist said he told the operations specialist that they had to get the fire contained and that until that time, there was nothing they could do. Both employees knew community emergency responders were waiting at the entrance of the compressor station.

The two men then drove toward the low-water crossing, proceeding down the right-of-way road toward the fire. The pipeline lead operations specialist later recalled that when they arrived at the location where they were going to try to close the block valves upstream of the fire, he carefully opened the door of his truck to confirm that he could tolerate the heat. About 6:05 a.m., the two employees left their vehicles and proceeded to the block valves. The pipeline lead operations specialist closed the No. 5 valve on line 1100, but closing this valve did not reduce the intensity of the fire. Together they closed block valve No. 6 on line 1103, and the operations specialist closed block valve No. 6 on line 1110. The fire's intensity was noticeably reduced after valve No. 6 on line 1103 was closed, but the fire continued to burn at the lowered intensity. The pipeline lead operations specialist told the operations specialist to check the bypass valve on the pig receiver[14] on line 1103 and after it was closed, the fire subsided altogether over a period of several minutes. At about 6:21 a.m., the pipeline lead operations specialist called the gas control center and reported the status of the valves and that the fire was out.

The pipeline lead operations specialist then told the operations specialist to go back to the west side of the river and prevent traffic from entering the area. The operations specialist said that as he passed where he thought he may have seen the vehicles during the fire, he now clearly saw burned pickup trucks. He stopped and called the pipeline lead operations specialist to tell him there were casualties. The pipeline lead operations specialist then notified his supervisor and told him to call for more ambulances.

The operations specialist took a first-aid kit from his truck and started down on foot to check on survivors. At this time, the station lead operations specialist pulled up behind his truck. He knew where the operations specialist was because he had been monitoring radio traffic. After the two men discussed the situation, the operations specialist went to assist the victims while the station lead operations specialist drove back to where he knew fire and emergency medical personnel were waiting. He then led an ambulance to the fire area. The pipeline lead operations specialist said he drove to the

---

[14] The *pig receiver* is an arrangement of pipe and valves connected to the pipeline that allows a pig to be removed from the pipeline.

location of the No. 6 3/4 block valves and, with the assistance of two other EPNG employees, closed a valve that double-blocked line 1110 (to prevent gas from entering the station in case one of the block valves on the line was leaking).

The station pipeline specialist had been called by the gas control center as soon as the Pecos River compressor station shut down at about 5:30 a.m. to determine if the problem was at the station. When he arrived at the entrance road to the compressor station off Whitethorn Road at about 6:10 a.m., he met the two operations specialists he had telephoned earlier and saw the Loving Fire Department vehicles on Whitethorn Road at the entrance driveway to the compressor station. He turned into the entrance road, entered the compressor station, and went to the control room to inspect the equipment. He said he knew that power was off at the station because no lights were available in the control room. He said that the automatic emergency shutdown system had vented gas from the station, shut off electrical service, and started the battery-powered cool-down pumps on the compressors. He and the two operations specialists then crossed the road to the 3191 block valve for the South Carlsbad line. This valve was just outside the east fence of the compressor station where line 3191 connects to lines 1103 and 1110. They finished closing the block valve at about 6:16 a.m., thereby isolating the South Carlsbad compressor station from the Pecos River station and from lines 1103 and 1110. The station lead operations specialist telephoned the gas control center and informed personnel there that the valve was closed and that the South Carlsbad compressor station should be taken off line. The station lead operations specialist sent the other two employees back to Whitethorn Road to help with crowd control as needed.

At about 5:51, the first emergency responders arrived on scene and staged on Whitethorn Road where the driveway into the Pecos River compressor station intersects the road. Additional emergency responders also staged at this location, which is about 3/4 mile from the accident site. The Carlsbad Fire Department's medic units had responded to the initial call and proceeded as far as the Pecos River compressor station. They remained there until an ambulance was directed to the victims and EPNG employees admitted the smaller fire vehicles.[15] When one of the fire engines entered the unpaved road from the west during the fire before the No. 6 block valves were closed, the station lead pipeline operations specialist stopped them from going farther. He told fireman to stand by while he shut more valves. As police cars arrived at that location, he told them to go back to the railroad tracks and let only EPNG vehicles or vehicles with flashing red lights through. Emergency vehicles were admitted as needed to the accident scene after the fire at the ruptured line was out.

The victims were camped about 675 feet from the crater, between the crater and the river. Emergency personnel located victims with the assistance of the operations specialist. Six victims were found at the camping area; six others had gone into the river and were either in the river or had been assisted to the banks by the operations specialist. Paramedics and emergency medical technicians worked to treat the injuries. Volunteer

---

[15] The station lead operations specialist was concerned that the larger fire fighting equipment would become stuck on the sandy access road.

firefighters and the crews of Carlsbad medic units then evacuated the six victims to hospital burn centers in Texas. None of the victims survived.

The New Mexico State Police responded to the accident and assumed responsibility for emergency management of the incident. Police personnel also provided support to Safety Board personnel during the on-scene investigation. EPNG reported the accident to the National Response Center at 8:27 a.m.

Pipeline Operations After the Rupture

EPNG gas controllers called gas suppliers to inform them of the problem and to request that gas supplies into the affected part of the EPNG system be reduced or suspended due to the incident and the immediate need to shut in all three lines. While only one pipeline ruptured, two other pipelines (1100 and 1110) near the rupture site were shut down and inspected for damage. All compressors at Keystone compressor station "A" plant, as well as Unit 3 at the Keystone compressor station "B" plant, which had been delivering gas toward the Pecos River, were off by 6:25 a.m.

Meanwhile, the gas control center was in the process of rebalancing the south pipeline system to compensate for the isolated Pecos River compressor station. At about 6:10 a.m., the gas control center directed personnel at the Washington Ranch storage facility[16] to stop injecting gas into the storage field and to begin withdrawing gas from the field. Withdrawing gas from storage allowed EPNG to continue to send gas west.

Postaccident On-Site Inspection

The force of the rupture and the violent ignition of the escaping gas created a 51-foot-wide crater about 113 feet along the pipe. A 49-foot section of the pipe was ejected from the crater in three pieces measuring approximately 3 feet, 20 feet, and 26 feet in length. (See figure 6.) The largest piece was found about 287 feet northwest of the crater in the direction of the suspension bridges. Investigators visually examined the pipeline that remained in the crater as well as the three ejected pieces. All three ejected pieces showed evidence of internal corrosion damage, but one of the pieces showed significantly more corrosion damage than the other two. Pits were visible on the inside surface of this piece, and at various locations, the pipe wall evidenced significant thinning. At one location, a through-wall perforation was visible. No significant corrosion damage was visible on the outside surfaces of the three pieces or on the two ends of the pipeline remaining in the crater. Pieces were cut from the ruptured pipeline segments and shipped to the Safety Board's Materials Laboratory in Washington, D.C., for further evaluation. (That evaluation is discussed in the "Tests and Research" section of this report.)

---

[16] Washington Ranch storage facility, an attended facility about 24 miles west and downstream of the Pecos River compressor station, received and delivered gas through lines 1100, 1103, and 1110.

Figure 6. Looking west at a portion of the crater created by the rupture. The missing section of pipe between the arrows was ejected from the crater.

The drip[17] between block valve No. 6 and the rupture site was removed from the pipeline and visually examined. The drip was found to contain a blackish oily-powdery/grainy material. At the area of its heaviest concentration, about 13 feet from the drip opening, this material filled approximately 70 percent of the cross-sectional area of the drip. No significant material was observed in the area just underneath and several inches away from the siphon drain at the closed end of the drip. No significant internal corrosion was observed in the drip.

Injuries

All 12 persons who were camping on the east bank of the Pecos River were fatally injured in the accident. The causes of death were extensive thermal burns, carbon monoxide poisoning, and smoke inhalation. (See table 1).

---

[17] The *drip* (described in more detail later in this report) was a 40-foot-long stub line that branched off the bottom of the gas pipeline. The drip was designed to collect liquids and solids that may have built up in the pipeline during normal transportation of gas or after pigging operations.

Table 1. Injuries

Injury Type	Public	Employees	Total
Fatal	12	0	12
Serious	0	0	0
Minor	0	0	0
Total	12	0	12

49 *Code of Federal Regulations* (CFR) 830.2 defines *fatal injury* as "any injury which results in death within 30 days of the accident" and *serious injury* as "an injury which: (1) requires hospitalization for more than 48 hours, commencing within 7 days from the date the injury was received; (2) results in a fracture of any bone (except simple fractures of fingers, toes, or nose); (3) causes severe hemorrhages, nerve, or tendon damage; (4) involves any internal organ; or (5) involves second- or third-degree burns, or any burn affecting more than 5 percent of the body surface."

Damages

Approximately 49 feet of the underground portion of line 1103 were ejected in three pieces from the crater created by the rupture. Two of the pieces of pipe were thrown 234 and 287 feet, respectively, from the northwest end of the crater toward the river. One of these pieces hit the cables that supported the pipeline suspension bridges across the river. The concrete anchor blocks for the cables, the cables themselves, and the two suspension bridge steel structures on the east side of the river were burned, as were the aboveground portions of the pipelines. The two pipelines that were being supported on the bridges (EPNG's 26-inch line 1100 and the out-of-service 16-inch line 1000) fell and came to rest on the ground on each side of the river, but neither leaked. The three vehicles and camping equipment on the east side of the river were destroyed, and vegetation along both riverbanks was burned. Based on photographs taken of the fire as it engulfed the suspension bridges, the height of the flame was calculated to be about 496 feet. EPNG, in its incident report to the Research and Special Programs Administration (RSPA), stated the cost of the accident was $998,296.

Toxicological Information

Specimens for drug testing were collected from the controllers and the coordinator on Sunday, August 20. The EPNG substance testing contractor, Behavioral Training Institute, Inc., performed the collections and forwarded the specimens to Universal Toxicology Laboratories in Midland, Texas. The results were reviewed by a medical review officer at SurgiMed, P.A., in El Paso, Texas. Tests were negative for the tested drugs.[18]

---

[18] Specimens were tested for marijuana, cocaine, opiates, amphetamines, and phencyclidine (PCP).

Tests and Research

Metallurgical Examination

On-site examination of the three pieces of pipe that were ejected from the crater at the rupture site identified severe internal corrosion along the interior bottom of the pipe. (See figure 7.) From these three segments, eight pieces were excised and transported to the Safety Board's Materials Laboratory in Washington, D.C., for further examination. The examination of these pieces revealed no evidence of corrosion on the outside of the pipe or the internal surface across the top half of the pipe (between the 9 and 3 o'clock positions looking downstream/west). Severe wall loss due to corrosion was observed on the inside of the pipe at the bottom.

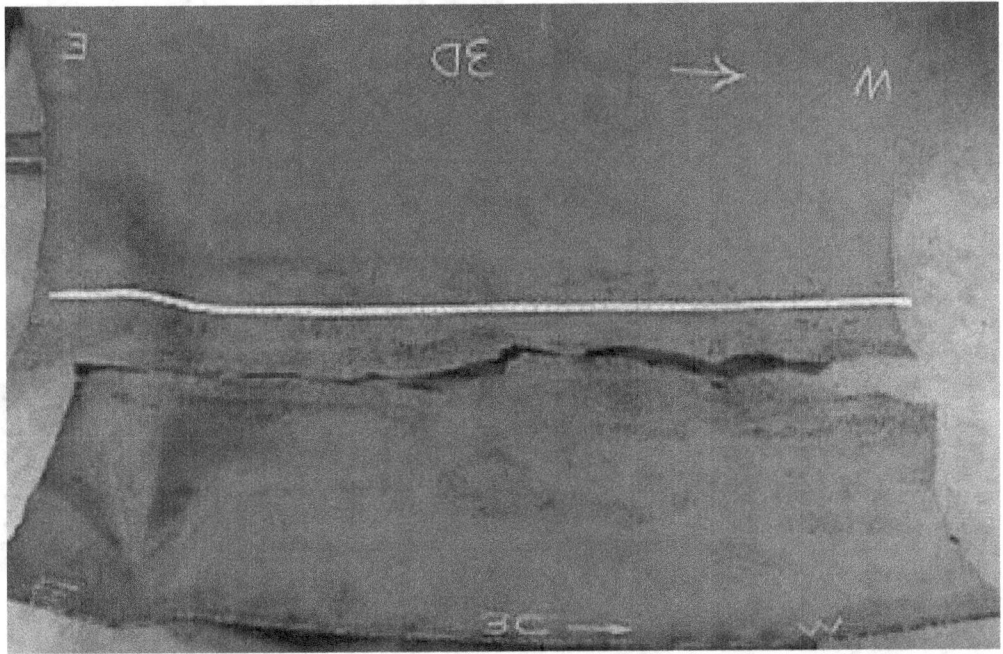

Figure 7. Fractured section of line 1103.

The area of corrosion damage extended 21 feet 5 inches. Sections of the girth (circumferential) and seam (longitudinal) welds that were in the bottom half of the pipe exhibited damage from internal corrosion similar to that found on the bottom pipe wall. The extent of corrosion damage (metal loss and number of pits) was most severe along the bottom of the pipe; the most severely corroded area reduced the original pipe wall thickness by 72 percent. (See figure 8.) The wall of many of the corrosion pits contained striations that extended around the pit. (See figure 9.) Within this length of corrosion damage were five circumferential wrinkles[19] in the pipe wall on the top of the pipe.

---

[19] A *wrinkle* is a smooth fold in the pipe wall that may have a single inward or single outward displacement or that may include a sinusoidal waveform with both inward and outward displacements. The five wrinkles in this pipe were outward deflections of the pipe wall.

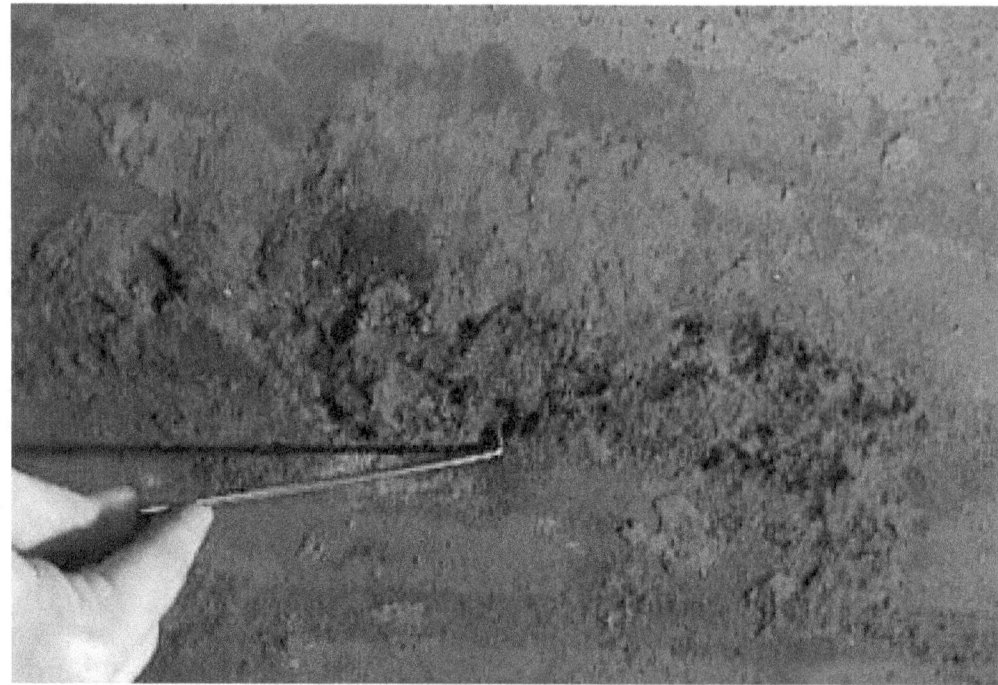

Figure 8. Corrosion pitting on inside of pipe near rupture site.

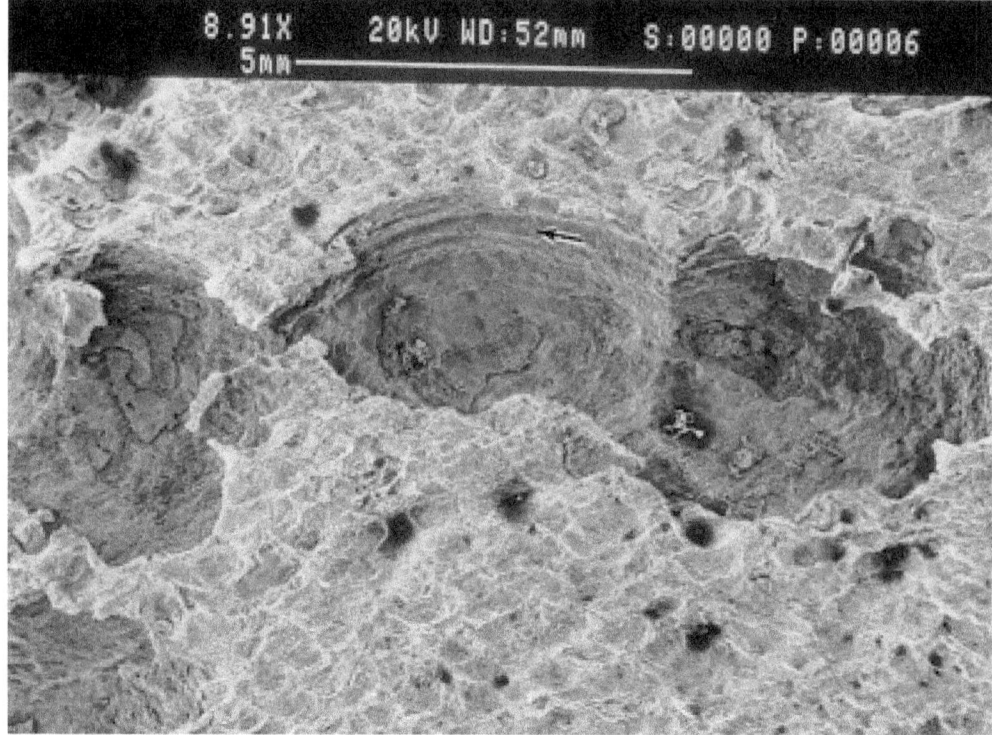

Figure 9. Microscopic view of corrosion pit showing striations

Examination of the fractures showed that a fracture face extended between the internal corrosion areas and the external wall of the pipe. The fracture faces resulted from overstress separation with no evidence of fatigue cracking or corrosion degradation, indicating that corrosion had not penetrated the wall of the pipe at the rupture point.

Corrosion Products

The Safety Board's Materials Laboratory performed x-ray dispersive spectroscopy analysis on material removed from corrosion pits and areas containing corrosion damage, both from the inside of the pipe. The analysis found high levels of chlorine and sodium in the material.

After the accident, corrosion products, deposits, and liquid samples were collected from various locations in the EPNG transmission system and subjected to chemical and microbial analysis. Sample collection locations included the Pecos River and Keystone compressor station inlet scrubbers, the line 1103 drip, the line 1103 pig receiver at valve No. 6, and the line 1100 pig receiver at valve No. 5. Anaerobic bacteria were present in all deposit/corrosion product samples, and aerobic bacteria were present in 9 of 11 samples; sulfate-reducing bacteria were detected in 18 of 22 individual tests (10 of 11 samples), and acid-producing bacteria were detected in 10 of 22 individual tests (7 of 11 samples). The chemical analysis indicated the presence of chlorides in all samples. Chloride concentrations exceeding 9,000 parts per million (ppm) were detected in three of four samples obtained from Line 1103. One of these three samples, obtained from the line 1103 pig receiver, showed a chloride concentration of 333,000 ppm, or roughly 33 percent of the sample. The fourth sample, collected from the line 1103 drip at a point away from the siphon drain, showed a chloride concentration of less than 50 ppm.

Samples taken from corrosion pits detected in line 1103 after the accident at a low point in the pipeline (about 2,080 feet downstream of the rupture site) showed positive reactions for all four types of bacteria (sulfate-reducing, acid-producing, anaerobic, and aerobic). At this location, the pipe contained a circumferential wrinkle across the top half of the pipe and corrosion on the internal surface of the bottom of the pipe.

Additional chemical and microbial tests were conducted by EPNG on samples collected from various transmission facilities. These data showed the presence of acid-producing bacteria in all samples obtained from the corrosion pit areas. Concentrations greater than 10,000 cells/ml of acid-producing bacteria were observed in 9 out of 13 samples obtained from various pit areas. Only 1 out of these 13 samples showed microbial concentration less than 10 cells/ml. Chloride levels of less than 100 ppm were observed in 26 of 85 samples. Chloride levels greater than 1,000 ppm were observed in 34 of 85 sludge/deposit samples. The highest observed chloride level was 400,000 ppm.

Chemical analyses showed that the pH of the liquid collected at the Pecos River compressor station plant inlet separator scrubber was 6.7 to 6.8. The pH of the liquid collected at the Keystone compressor station inlet scrubber was 8.2. For the material collected at the line 1100 and 1103 pig receivers, the pH level was 6.2 to 6.3. The pH of the inside material collected from a low spot on line 1103 west of the rupture was 6.4.

Analysis of the material collected near the siphon drain area of the line 1103 drip showed a pH of 8.9.

Chlorides were observed in all corrosion product/deposit samples. The morphology of corrosion damage located away from the bottom of the ruptured pipe appeared similar to water line corrosion.

Pipeline 1103

At the time of the accident, EPNG operated more than 10,000 miles of natural gas transmission pipelines involving 59 compressor stations and plants and more than 300 compressor units. The company operated three of the four in-service gas pipelines at the Pecos River crossing, including line 1103, the pipeline that ruptured in this accident.

The section of pipeline 1103 between the Keystone compressor station and the Pecos River compressor station was constructed in 1950 with pipe purchased from Republic Steel that had been manufactured in accordance with American Petroleum Institute standard 5LX, High-Test Line Pipe (first edition, 1948). The pipe was 30-inch outside diameter (OD), grade X52 (specified minimum yield strength of 52,000 psi[20]) pipe with a nominal wall thickness of 0.335 inch, with sections of heavier wall pipe at locations such as road crossings and block valve assemblies. The longitudinal seam weld in the pipe was a double submerged arc weld. The pipeline was cathodically protected, and the coating was coal-tar wrap.

The pipeline was operating at approximately 675 pounds per square inch, gauge (psig), at the time of the accident. The maximum allowable operating pressure from Keystone compressor station to the Pecos River compressor station had been established by EPNG at 837 psig.[21]

Pipeline Features

Valves. Block valves were spaced along line 1103 between the Keystone and Pecos River compressor stations at intervals ranging from 1 mile to 19.2 miles. From the rupture location, block valve No. 6 at the pig receiver was the closest upstream/east valve (0.25 mile), and block valve No. 6 1/2 at the Pecos River compressor station was the closest downstream/west valve (0.85 mile).

When pigging facilities, including the pig receiver, were installed in the mid-1970s, the valve then designated block valve No. 6 (a 30-inch gate valve) became the receiver isolation valve. A new plug valve was installed in the bypass around the pig

---

[20] Although yield strength is expressed in pounds per square inch, this number is an expression of the pipe material strength value, which is not equivalent to a pipe's internal pressure.

[21] Equivalent to a stress level of 72 percent of specified minimum yield strength in the 0.335-inch-wall-thickness pipe.

receiver and was designated block valve No. 6. Block valve No. 6 was 0.25 mile upstream/east of the rupture site.

Line 1103 was cross-connected with other lines upstream of the rupture site as follows:

- Lines 1103 and 1110 were cross-connected in three places between the Keystone and Pecos River compressor stations upstream/east of the rupture site.

- Lines 1103 and 1100 were cross-connected between block valve No. 6 and the line 1103 drip.

Crossover to Line 1100. About 720 feet downstream/west of block valve No. 6, a 16-inch OD crossover (branch line with valves) cross-connected lines 1103 and 1100. The crossover was installed during the original construction of the pipeline. Line 1100 was equipped with a drip until 1989, at which time the drip was found to be "completely full of solidified black solids & oil" and was removed. No internal corrosion was observed.

Line 1103 Drip Assembly. About 990 feet downstream/west of block valve No. 6 was a drip, a liquid collection leg buried beneath the pipeline that consisted of about 40 feet of 30-inch pipe. (See figure 10.) The leg was buried approximately 7 feet directly below the gas pipeline and sloped downward toward a dead end equipped with a siphon drain. The leg functioned to collect liquids and solids during normal transportation or after pigging operations. Also at this location was a liquid storage tank consisting of a 4,620-gallon aboveground steel tank installed within a concrete dike. The siphon drain in the liquid collection leg of the drip assembly emptied into this tank. (See figure 11.) The tank was fitted with piping and valves for loading the collected liquids into a truck for disposal. The drip assembly was installed during the original construction of the pipeline. Because of the location and design of this drip, cleaning pigs could not be run in the section of pipeline that ruptured. After the removal of the line 1100 drip in 1989, liquids and solids moving down line 1100 toward the Pecos River compressor station during both normal operations and pigging operations in line 1100 could enter line 1103 upstream of the drip.

Pecos River Crossing. About 2,025 feet downstream/west of block valve No. 6 was a steel bridge with a single-lane concrete service road spanning approximately 430 feet across the Pecos River. Pipeline 1103 rested on, and was strapped to, horizontal steel support members off the side of the north bridge girders.

Gas Suppliers

Line 1103. In addition to receiving gas from the Keystone compressor station, line 1103 had been connected to and received gas from other gas suppliers beginning in 1979. Seven receipt points existed between the Keystone and Pecos River compressor stations where gas flowed into the line for periods ranging from 6 months to 21 years, but at the time of the accident, only one active supplier, an interstate transmission pipeline, was connected to line 1103.

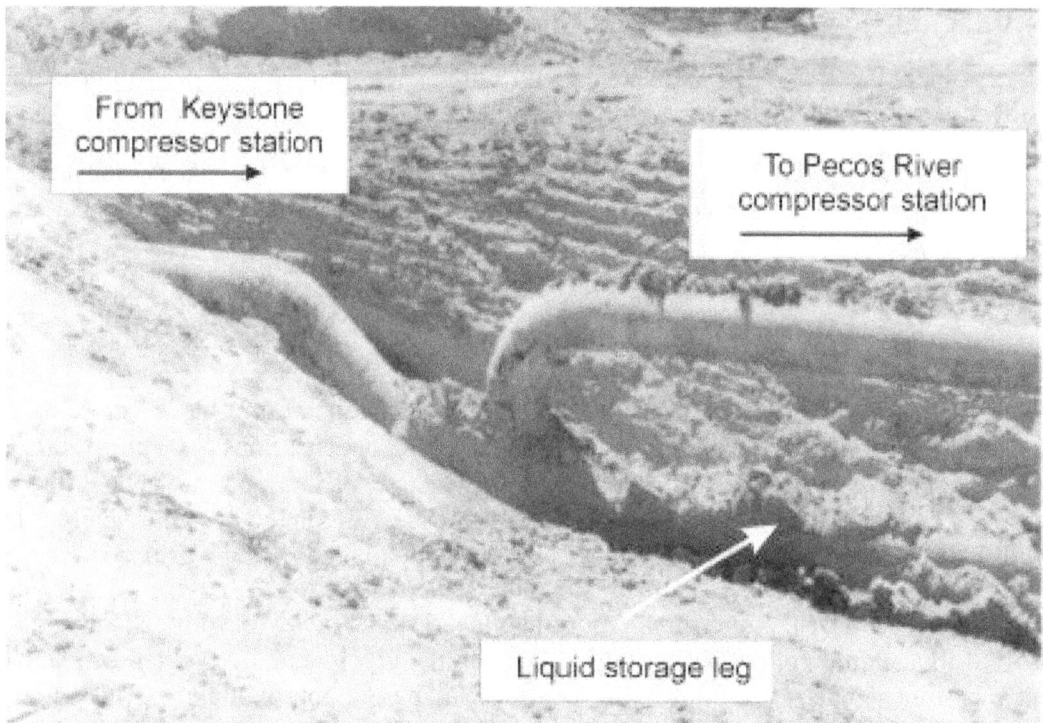

Figure 10. Line 1103 drip after excavation.

Line 1110. In addition to the gas entering line 1110 from its connection with line 1103, two receipt points flowed gas into line 1110 beginning in 1979 for periods of 14 years and 21 years, respectively. At the time of the accident, only one active supplier, the same interstate transmission pipeline connected to line 1103, was connected to line 1110.

Line 1100. In addition to the gas entering line 1100 from the EPNG's Eunice plant, 25 receipt points flowed gas into line 1100 beginning in 1949 for periods ranging from 1 1/2 years to 51 years. At the time of the accident, 11 active suppliers were connected to line 1100.

Pigging Operations

When pigging facilities were added to line 1103 about 25 years after initial construction, a pig launcher was installed at block valve No. 2 approximately 10.5 miles downstream/west of the Keystone compressor station, and a pig receiver was installed at block valve No. 6. At the time of the accident, the line could be pigged from block valve No. 2 to block valve No. 6. The line was pigged to remove solids and liquids that had collected in the pipeline. According to EPNG, when possible, cleaning pigs were run a minimum of twice per year.

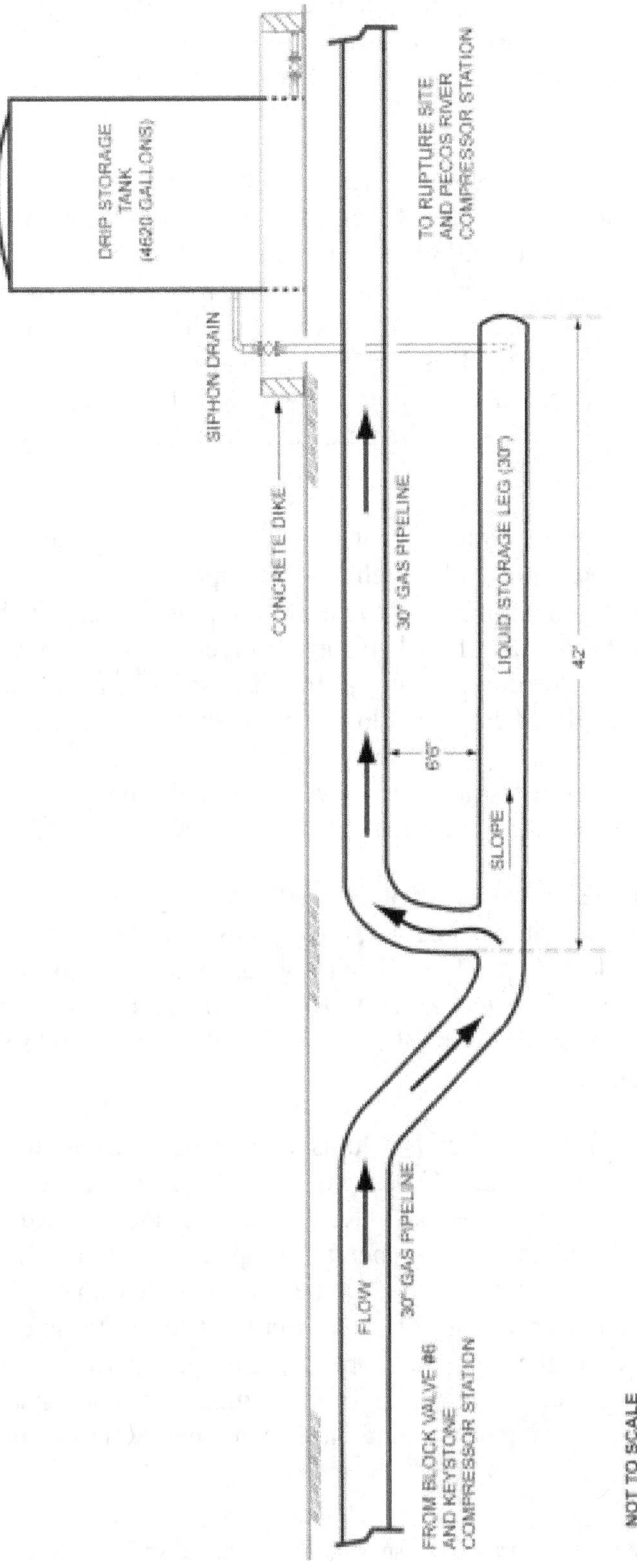

Figure 11. Diagram of line 1103 drip.

There was no pig launcher at block valve No. 6 and no pig receiver at Pecos River compressor station. For that reason, and because of a reduced port valve[22] and other pipeline features, including the drip, in the section of the pipeline between block valve No. 6 and the Pecos River compressor station, that portion of the pipeline (which included the rupture location) could not be pigged.

At the time of the accident, the design of the pipeline was such that liquids and solids not caught at the pig receiver at block valve No. 6 would continue downstream past the block valve assembly to the drip downstream/west of the block valve. EPNG officials said gas pressure in the drip was used to blow the material out of the drip after each pigging operation, causing the materials to move to the adjacent, aboveground storage tank for later removal by truck. This tank was also used in conjunction with the drip on line 1110. Officials said that in addition to being emptied after a pigging operation, drips were blown on the 1st and 17th of each month, although the company did not keep records of blowdowns.

According to EPNG, material that remained in the pig receiver after a pigging operation was blown into a dirt pit through a 6-inch pipe off the bottom of the pig receiver near the closure. This 6-inch pipe also connected to an identical 6-inch pipe, which was used to blow down the adjacent line 1110 pig receiver into the same disposal pit. After about 1975, the 6-inch blowdown piping to the disposal pit was taken out of service. A concrete basin was installed below the closure at the end of the pig receiver, and pigging residue was removed from the pig receiver via the closure and transferred to portable fiberglass containers for disposal. There were no drain lines or liquid storage legs connected to the pig receiver, as the downstream drip served to collect the pig liquids.

In the 3 years before the accident, line 1103 was pigged from near block valve No. 2 to block valve No. 6 four times in 1997, three times in 1998, once in 1999, and once in 2000 before the accident. Records for each pig run noted "no solids/liquids reported," except for the 1999 cleaning, for which "2100 lbs solid/2 barrels oil" was reported. In 2001, EPNG notified both RSPA and the Safety Board that the 1999 report of "2100 lbs" was more likely "20 lbs."

According to EPNG officials, fluids and sludge recovered after the pigging operations were sent to the EPNG laboratory in El Paso, Texas, and analyzed for hazardous components before disposal. Results of the analysis were provided to the complex manager and to the environmental compliance engineer responsible for the complex. Test results were also provided to the principal coordinator, corrosion services, and retained at the laboratory. The materials were not tested to determine if they were potentially corrosive to the pipeline. The laboratory superintendent for the EPNG chemistry laboratory stated that samples from pigging and other inspections had water concentrations ranging from trace amounts (less than 1 percent) to 10 percent.

---

[22] The opening in a *reduced port valve* is smaller than the actual valve size, which prevents a pig from passing through the valve. For example, the passage through a 30-inch valve could be a 24-inch-diameter opening.

At the Pecos River compressor station, four inlet scrubbers removed liquids from the gas stream entering the station from lines 1100, 1103, and 1110. The collected liquids were analyzed in the same manner as pig liquids. The materials were not tested to determine if they were potentially corrosive to the pipeline.

In July 1997, because of a recent rupture of line 1300 due to internal corrosion, EPNG conducted an in-line inspection (using a "smart pig" internal inspection tool) of a 70-mile section of line 1300. According to EPNG, this inspection found no areas of internal corrosion requiring repair, but a visual inspection of the pipeline in the immediate area of the rupture found an area of internal corrosion, which was repaired. In June and July 1998, 33 miles of line 1103 and 33 miles of line 1100, which included a segment of pipe in which a rupture had recently occurred, were inspected with an in-line inspection tool. The inspected segments of lines 1100 and 1103 were downstream of the Pecos River compressor station. No areas of internal corrosion requiring repair were discovered. In February 2000, EPNG conducted in-line inspections of 33 miles of lines 3133/3137 upstream of Goldsmith Plant in Texas. No areas of internal corrosion requiring repair were discovered.

Tests and Inspections

The line 1103 right-of-way had most recently (before the accident) been inspected on August 11, 2000, by aerial patrol and on August 18, 2000, by ground patrol. Inspectors looked for evidence of leaks (such as discolored soil or dying vegetation), erosion, and excavation near the pipeline. No leaks were reported.

Before the accident, the segment of line 1103 between the Pecos River and Keystone compressor stations had never been internally inspected, nor had it been pressure-tested except for two segments, totaling approximately 0.9 mile located approximately 46 miles upstream of the rupture location, that had been hydrostatically tested.[23]

EPNG's Internal Corrosion Program

According to EPNG, before the accident, the company monitored and mitigated internal corrosion by controlling the quality of gas entering the pipeline, by visually inspecting the inside of exposed pipe (and, under certain conditions, performing an ultrasound test to determine pipe wall thickness), by running cleaning pigs through the pipeline to remove liquids, and by blowing down the drips to remove the liquids and to verify that the drips were functioning properly. EPNG officials stated that they believed that line 1103 was not transporting corrosive gas because the line was receiving "pipeline

---

[23] Current Federal regulations require that gas pipelines be pressure-tested before being placed in service. These requirements did not exist when line 1103 was constructed, and when the regulations were issued later, the requirements for pressure-testing did not apply to existing pipelines.

quality" gas and that unusual conditions, such as water in the pipeline, were not being observed at the pig receiver or the drip on line 1103.

Gas quality standards were contained in EPNG's contracts with its gas suppliers but were not referenced in the company's corrosion control procedures. Some interconnect locations had gas quality monitoring, which either closed a valve to stop the flow of gas into the transmission pipeline or alarmed in the gas control center if the limit of any specified contaminant was exceeded. Not all contaminants were monitored at each monitoring location.

For line 1103, gas quality monitoring was installed in the discharge of the Keystone compressor station, at the suction to the Pecos River compressor station, and at the receipt point with the interstate transmission pipeline approximately 17 miles downstream/west of the Keystone compressor station. This interconnect location had an automatic closing valve (referred to as a "slam valve") actuated by high levels of hydrogen sulfide (H_2S), and an alarm actuated by high levels of carbon dioxide (CO_2). No slam valves or alarms were installed at any of the other receipt locations in line 1103 between the Keystone and Pecos River compressor stations.

EPNG was not able to provide water vapor data for line 1103 at the discharge from the Keystone compressor station for 19 months between 1998 and 2000.[24] At this same location, records showed that moisture monitoring instrument readings remained unchanged from July 10 to 16, 1992; October 1 to 18, 1994; August 13 to 25 and 27 to 30, 1998. The moisture monitoring instrument at the Pecos River compressor station inlet also showed unchanged readings from July 11 to 17, 1991; June 16 to July 26, 1994; June 28 to July 28 and August 1 to 25, 1996. Similarly, moisture monitoring instruments at the Pecos River compressor station inlet for lines 1100 and 1110 showed periods of unchanged readings.

For line 1110, gas quality monitoring was installed in the suction to the Pecos River compressor station and at the receipt point with the interstate transmission pipeline approximately 17 miles downstream/west of the Keystone compressor station. This interconnect location had a slam valve actuated by high levels of H_2S and an alarm actuated by high levels of CO_2. At the other receipt location on line 1110 between Keystone and Pecos River compressor stations, there was a slam valve actuated by high levels of H_2S and an alarm actuated by high levels of CO_2.

For line 1100 between Eunice plant and the Pecos River compressor station, gas quality monitoring was installed on the suction to the Pecos River compressor station. Two of the 26 receipt locations between Eunice plant and the Pecos River compressor station had slam valves actuated by high levels of H_2S and alarms actuated by high levels of CO_2. In the event of an alarm, gas control center personnel notified the pipeline location supervisor and a technician would be called out to investigate. The remaining receipt locations were not equipped with slam valves or alarms.

---

[24] EPNG officials advised the Safety Board that they believed that the monitoring instrumentation was working, but that the data were not recorded electronically.

EPNG officials said that at other locations, its personnel periodically (at 1- to 6-month intervals) sampled and analyzed the gas entering the pipeline. There were no written requirements that corrosion technicians follow up on reports of out-of-specification gas being received or identify the effect, if any, of this gas on the pipeline. Corrosion coupons[25] or corrosion monitoring devices were not used in this section of line 1103 because, officials said, the gas was not believed to be corrosive. EPNG did not inject any corrosion inhibitors into line 1103. The program did not require that ultrasonic testing be performed on the low points of the non-piggable portions of line 1103, and none was performed before the accident. According to EPNG, visual inspections of line 1103 in the area of the Keystone and Pecos River compressor stations that were exposed during operations or maintenance activities before the accident had not shown evidence of internal corrosion.

Internal Corrosion Control Procedures

Procedures in Effect Before the Accident. Although at the time of the accident, EPNG was in the process of implementing updated internal corrosion procedures (discussed below), the company's internal corrosion control program in the period leading up to the rupture was governed by its *Operating and Maintenance Procedures* manual. Section 201.2, "Corrosion Control," dated September 20, 1999, prescribed the minimum company requirements for monitoring and protecting metallic structures. The indicated references were 49 *Code of Federal Regulations* (CFR) 192.451 through 192.491, which include Federal regulations regarding internal corrosion. Most of Section 201.2 related to external corrosion. Requirements for an internal corrosion program were as follows:

> If corrosive gas is transported or if internal corrosion is found, Corrosion Services will recommend the appropriate corrective action and establish an internal corrosion monitoring program to determine the effectiveness of mitigation programs. Internal corrosion mitigation will continue until monitoring and testing determines that the source of corrosion has been removed or other corrective actions have rendered the gas stream non-corrosive. Internal monitoring will be performed at least twice each calendar year, but with intervals not to exceed 7 1/2 months. Additional monitoring will be performed if necessary. A Remedial Action Form will be completed if internal corrosion is discovered on any portion of the pipeline or ancillary components and vessels containing natural gas.

> Each time a pipeline or station pipe segment is exposed for any reason, the coating and pipe will be evaluated and documented. Whenever any pipe is removed from a pipeline, it shall be inspected for internal corrosion. If internal corrosion is found, the adjacent pipe must be investigated to determine its extent and appropriate measures taken as detailed in these procedures.

---

[25] A *corrosion coupon* is a small piece of metal with a specially prepared surface for measuring corrosion rates. Corrosion coupons may be inserted into the pipeline during pipeline operations to help operators assess the potential for internal corrosion or to evaluate the effectiveness of corrosion mitigation efforts.

The procedures did not address the factors that should be considered in determining whether the gas being transported could cause corrosion. The company stated that the company's gas quality standard, set forth in its contracts, addressed several contaminants, including water, CO_2, H_2S, and oxygen (O_2), but the corrosion control procedures did not reference these contaminants or their acceptable limits. In the event that it was determined that corrosive gas was being transported or internal corrosion was occurring, corrosion-mitigation actions would be taken. But the procedures did not detail how technicians were to carry out semi-annual monitoring to determine if the corrosion mitigation measures were effective. The procedures did not provide guidance regarding how internal corrosion would be detected other than through visual inspection of a pipe segment after it had been removed.

Procedures in Effect at the Time of the Accident. EPNG acquired Tenneco Energy in December 1996 and formed El Paso Energy Corporation. In January 2000, El Paso Energy Corporation acquired Sonat, Inc., another natural gas pipeline company.[26] El Paso Energy Corporation then assembled teams of representatives from each pipeline company and tasked them with establishing best practices and producing a common operating and maintenance manual. This new manual was issued on May 15, 2000. The new *Corrosion Control Manual*, which detailed the requirements for internal corrosion control and monitoring, was issued on July 10, 2000.

The section of the *Corrosion Control Manual* applicable to internal corrosion control was Section 700, "Internal Corrosion Control." The applicable sections of the *Operating and Maintenance Procedures* manual were Sections 308.1, "Corrosion, General and Records," and 308.3, "Internal Corrosion Control." References included in these sections were 49 CFR 192.453, 192.475, and 192.477, which address Federal requirements for internal corrosion control and monitoring.

Section 308.3 of the manual required that gas and liquids be tested to determine if they are corrosive and required further steps to minimize the possibility of internal corrosion. Section 700 of the *Corrosion Control Manual* included a statement that quality standards for gas and liquids entering the pipeline represent the first line of defense against internal corrosion and noted that only by regular monitoring and analysis can it be determined if a pipeline is carrying corrosive gas. Detailed descriptions in section 700 for sampling procedures indicate that sampling and analysis of gas, liquids, and solids removed from the pipeline is required.

Section 700 also contained a discussion of corrosive constituents in gas streams; listed the company's typical gas and liquid quality standards, velocity standards, and corrosion coupon and inhibitor guidelines; schedules for pipeline liquid, gas, and solid sampling; and requirements for preservation of evidence after a leak or failure. Also noted in the documents was that water and other corrosives may enter the pipeline by accident or may gradually accumulate in low spots despite gas quality monitoring that shows

---

[26] After acquiring Coastal Corporation in January 2001, El Paso Energy Corporation became El Paso Corporation. The El Paso Corporation pipeline system now consists of more than 46,000 miles of gas transmission pipelines.

adherence to quality standards. It also included the basic regulatory requirements that corrosive gas may not be transported by pipeline unless the effect of the gas on the pipeline has been investigated and steps have been taken to minimize internal corrosion; that the internal surface of a pipeline be inspected whenever the pipe is exposed and opened; and that coupons or other means be used to determine the effectiveness of the steps taken to minimize internal corrosion.

Before July 10, 2000, the EPNG operating and maintenance standards did not address the relationship of flow velocity to liquid accumulation in a pipeline. The *Corrosion Control Manual* dated July 10, 2000, included a velocity standards subsection that stated the velocity of wet gas (defined as gas containing more water vapor than the amount specified, typically 7 pounds of water per million standard cubic feet of gas) in a pipeline must be limited to avoid solids-erosion or erosion-corrosion. The procedure required that consideration be given to flow patterns in the pipeline when evaluating liquid transported by gas. Flow patterns were described for velocities less than 7.5 feet per second (dormant pools in a dry gas stream occur), 7.5 to 15 feet per second (agitated pools and minor spray occur), 15 to 25 feet per second (continuous stream along the bottom of the pipe, small agitated pools, and spray occur), and greater than 25 feet per second (no liquids, only spray occurs).

Gas velocity data provided by EPNG for the period 1991 to 2001 indicates that gas velocities in line 1103 ranged from 2 to 33 feet per second. Typical velocities ranged from a low of 2 to 7 feet per second to a high of 15 to 23 between 1993 and 2000, with velocities as high as 33 feet per second in 1991 and 1992.

At the time of the rupture, El Paso Energy was in the process of implementing the July 10, 2000, corrosion procedures in Section 700 of the *Corrosion Control Manual* and had conducted a training session for corrosion technicians in El Paso during the first week of August 2000. Other personnel assigned corrosion control responsibilities were scheduled for training at a later date.

After the accident, EPNG revised the sections of the *Operating and Maintenance Procedures* and the *Corrosion Control Manual* that affect internal corrosion control. EPNG's current manual (*Corrosion Control Manual*, Section 6, effective December 31, 2001) states "identification of corrosive gas in a pipeline is achieved by analysis of operating conditions, gas impurity content, monitoring data, mitigation schemes, and/or other considerations" and that "an effective internal corrosion-monitoring program includes sampling and analysis of liquid, gas and solid materials."

Internal Audit Program

EPNG's *Quality Assurance Auditing Procedures Manual* (February 4, 1999, revised March 3, 1999) describes the company's internal audit program. For internal corrosion, the pipeline and plant/stations sections of the manual have a section entitled "Corrosion Control–Internal Coupons." Answers to the following questions are required for the audit:

Is corrosive gas being transported? If so, has the effect of the gas on the pipeline been investigated? What steps have been taken to minimize internal corrosion? Corrosion inhibitor? Dehydration? Have internal coupons been installed to monitor the effectiveness of the corrosion-mitigating program? If so, are the coupons checked two times each calendar year at intervals not exceeding 7-1/2 months? Is the mil loss per year acceptable?

Preprinted forms were provided in the manual for the auditor to record the results of an internal audit. For pipelines, these forms did not list the internal corrosion items identified in the audit questions or provide a space for the auditor to document the results of the internal corrosion portion of the audit.

An EPNG senior safety staff member who conducted internal audits told investigators that auditors relied on the location manager/superintendent to tell them whether or not corrosive gas was being transported through the pipeline. This employee stated that he was aware that gas quality specifications existed, but he did not know what they were or what EPNG would consider to be corrosive gas per these specifications. In September 1996, EPNG's line 1300 ruptured because of internal corrosion. The senior safety staff member stated that previous internal audits had not found indications that internal corrosion may be occurring in line 1300 or that the use of corrosion coupons or other monitoring methods were needed in the line. In addition, he stated that after the rupture of line 1300, the internal audit program was not revised.

Regulatory Oversight

Federal Safety Standards

RSPA promulgates regulations that establish minimum standards for the transportation of natural gas by pipeline. The regulations for internal corrosion control for gas transmission pipelines in effect at the time of the accident are in 49 CFR Part 192, "Transportation of Natural and Other Gas by Pipeline: Minimum Federal Safety Standards," as follows:

Subpart L, 192.605 Procedural manual for operations, maintenance, and emergencies

Each operator shall include the following in its operating and maintenance plan:

(a) General. Each operator shall prepare and follow for each pipeline, a manual of written procedures for conducting operations and maintenance activities and for emergency response. For transmission lines, the manual must also include procedures for handling abnormal operations. This manual must be reviewed and updated by the operator at intervals not exceeding 15 months, but at least once each calendar year. This manual must be prepared before operations of a pipeline system commence. Appropriate parts of the manual must be kept at locations where operations and maintenance activities are conducted.

(b) Maintenance and normal operations. The manual required by paragraph (a) of this section must include procedures for the following, if applicable, to provide safety during maintenance and operations.

> (1) Operating, maintaining, and repairing the pipeline in accordance with each of the requirements of this subpart and Subpart M of this part.

> (2) Controlling corrosion in accordance with the operations and maintenance requirements of Subpart I of this part.

Subpart I, 192.453 General:

The corrosion control procedures required by §192.605(b)(2), including those for the design, installation, operation, and maintenance of cathodic protection systems, must be carried out by, or under the direction of, a person qualified in pipeline corrosion control methods.

192.475 Internal corrosion control: General:

Corrosive gas may not be transported by pipeline, unless the corrosive effect of the gas on the pipeline has been investigated and steps have been taken to minimize internal corrosion.

Whenever any pipe is removed from a pipeline for any reason, the internal surface must be inspected for evidence of corrosion. If internal corrosion is found, (1) The adjacent pipe must be investigated to determine the extent of internal corrosion; (2) Replacement must be made to the extent required by the applicable paragraphs of §§192.485, 192.487 or 192,489; and, (3) Steps must be taken to minimize the internal corrosion.

Gas containing more than 0.25 grain of hydrogen sulfide per 100 standard cubic feet (5.8 milligrams/m3) at standard conditions (4 parts per million) may not be stored in pipe-type or bottle-type holders.

Subpart I, 192.477 Internal corrosion control: Monitoring:

If corrosive gas is being transported, coupons or other suitable means must be used to determine the effectiveness of the steps taken to minimize internal corrosion. Each coupon or other means of monitoring internal corrosion must be checked two times each calendar year, but with intervals not exceeding 7 1/2 months.

The Federal pipeline safety regulations do not include design, construction, operating, or maintenance requirements that address the relationship of water and corrosive contaminants to internal corrosion in a gas pipeline.

Preaccident Federal Inspections of EPNG

From June 1990 to August 1998, RSPA's Office of Pipeline Safety (OPS) conducted 18 safety inspections of EPNG. Inspections were conducted using a question-and-answer format. Four of these inspections were performed by personnel from the Arizona State Corporation Commission, as an agent for the OPS for interstate pipelines. For each of these 18 inspections, compliance with the internal corrosion control regulations was noted as "satisfactory" or, for items associated with corrosion coupons, "N/A" (not applicable). These inspections were based on an inspection form that typically had six questions related to internal corrosion: (1) Are corrosion control procedures established? (2) Are these procedures under the responsibility of a qualified person? (3) Have coupons been utilized and checked at least twice annually, not to exceed 7.5 months? (4) Is gas tested to determine corrosive properties? (5) Whenever a pipe segment is removed from a pipeline, is it examined for evidence of internal corrosion? (6) Remedial action (if required) to minimize internal corrosion? In each of the inspections, "satisfactory" was entered in response to question 4 regarding testing the gas for corrosive properties.

In December 1998, the OPS launched a 3-year pilot program designated the "system integrity inspection pilot program." EPNG applied for the program in February 1999, and after reviewing EPNG's qualifications, the OPS accepted EPNG into the program in April 2000. The system integrity inspection pilot program demonstration period expired at the end of 2001, at which time the program was terminated by the OPS. EPNG remained in the program until that time. The pilot program was an attempt by the OPS to develop a method by which the agency could ensure that a pipeline operator had an effective, compliance-driven internal audit plan and that the plan was effectively implemented. The program was intended to improve communication and information-sharing between operators and Government and to focus resources on the most important risks to pipeline safety.

From July 1999 to September 2000, the OPS conducted eight safety inspections of EPNG under the system integrity inspection pilot program. For each of these eight inspections, compliance with the internal corrosion control regulations was noted as "satisfactory" or "N/A." There were four internal corrosion related questions on the inspection report form used for six inspections, and they all were noted "satisfactory": (1) Does the company maintain a comprehensive corrosion control program and associated records? (2) Is the company's corrosion program under the direction of a qualified person, with associated records? (3) Are corrosion control procedures in place and do they follow Part 192/National Association of Corrosion Engineers (NACE)/industry standards, with associated records? (4) How is the gathered information reviewed and analyzed? Associated records? OPS memos summarizing several of these inspections noted that EPNG's internal audit program was working as designed.

One of these eight inspections was a joint team operation and maintenance procedures inspection conducted in April 2000. The form used for this inspection included four questions related to internal corrosion. The first was for the operator's procedure for internal corrosion control coupon monitoring (rated "Satisfactory"); the second was for the operator's procedure for corrosion remedial measures (rated "Satisfactory"); the third was for the records of the coupon monitoring (rated "Not Applicable"); and the fourth was for records of the corrosion control remedial measures (rated "Not Applicable"). There were no questions or subject areas on the inspection record related to transporting corrosive gas, the training of internal corrosion control personnel, or the qualifications of the person directing the internal corrosion control program, as required by 49 CFR 192.453. The OPS summary of this inspection did not identify any deficiencies in internal corrosion monitoring and control or personnel training. Before August 2000, there were no enforcement actions against EPNG for its internal corrosion program.

After the accident, the OPS revised the inspection form to include more detailed questions about internal corrosion. The revised form[27] has the following written guidance for the inspector:

- Proper procedures for transporting corrosive gas?

- Is pipe inspected for internal corrosion? If found: is adjacent pipe inspected? Is pipe replaced if required? Are steps taken to minimize internal corrosion?

- Internal corrosion control coupon monitoring (2 times per year / 7 1/2 months)

- The operator should maintain a comprehensive internal corrosion control program that includes the following (Best Practice):

- Sufficient fluid sample locations throughout their system for monitoring for corrosive elements.

- Does the operator have established threshold limits for various corrosive compounds in their procedures?

- Has the operator identified low points throughout their system where fluids are likely to accumulate and does the operator identify how to remove the fluids from the lines?

- Does the operator specify the frequency in how often the fluids are removed?

- Does the operator address fluid accumulation in unpiggable lines? (i.e., fluid samples, coupons, etc.) (Note: Refer to Advisory Bulletin ADB-00-02, 8/29/00; *Internal Corrosion of Gas Pipelines*).

Federal Safety Standards and Enforcement—Maps and Records

The Federal regulations for construction records, maps, and operating history for gas transmission pipelines in effect at the time of the accident are in 49 CFR Part 192, Subpart L, 192.605, Procedural Manual for Operations, Maintenance, and Emergencies, which includes the following:

(b) Maintenance and normal operations: The manual required by paragraph (a) of this section must include procedures for the following, if applicable, to provide safety during maintenance and operations:

(1) ....

---

[27] OPS Form-1 (192-90), "Evaluation Report of Gas Transmission Pipeline," (Revised 2/01/02 through amendment 192-90).

(2) ....

(3) Making construction records, maps, and operating history available to appropriate operating personnel.

For the 26 safety inspections of EPNG (referenced earlier) conducted by the OPS from June 1990 to September 2000, compliance with 192.605(b)(3) was noted as "satisfactory," "not applicable," "not checked," or, in some cases, the inspection form did not include questions specifically related to maps and records.

Before August 2000, there were no enforcement actions against EPNG for their program for making construction records, maps, and operating history available to operating personnel.

Postaccident Actions

Pipeline Reconstruction

After the accident, EPNG reconstructed lines 1103 and 1110 in the area of the river crossing. Line 1103 was modified to make it piggable between the Keystone and Pecos River compressor stations. During hydrostatic testing, line 1103 failed about 2,097 feet downstream/west of the accident site between the Pecos River and the Pecos River compressor station. At the failure location, pitting was observed on the internal surface of the bottom of the pipe, and the wall thickness had been reduced by approximately 69 percent. A March 2001 in-line inspection of line 1103, which included the segment in which cleaning pigs had been periodically run (from block valve No. 2 to block valve No. 6) found no areas of internal corrosion that required repair under the internal inspection analysis protocol developed by EPNG and reviewed by the OPS.

Line 1110 was modified to make it piggable from its beginning point on line 1103 to the Pecos River compressor station. EPNG investigated nine low points in line 1110 between its beginning point on line 1103 and the Pecos River compressor station. No indications of internal corrosion were found. Some of these low points were in the section of line 1110 upstream of block valve No. 6 in which cleaning pigs had been periodically run.

Line 1100 was removed from the suspension bridge, and new 26-inch pipe was constructed across the Pecos River and supported off the service bridge. Line 1000, which previously had been abandoned, was removed. The suspension bridges were removed and not replaced. EPNG modified the power supply to the SCADA computers and modem at Pecos River compressor station so that an emergency shutdown would not cause a loss of power to the local SCADA computer and modem.

Pipeline Integrity Management

After the accident, EPNG contracted for the development of a program to train company personnel in internal corrosion. According to EPNG, that program has been completed and implemented.

In response to the August 23, 2000, corrective action order (discussed in more detail below), EPNG identified 60 segments of pipeline where the risk of internal corrosion was judged to be the greatest. These segments were inspected by in-line inspection or other non-destructive means with the result that internal corrosion was discovered in eight pipelines. In six of these lines, the company judged the corrosion to be isolated instances. EPNG sent sections of the remaining two pipelines to the company's metallurgical laboratory for analysis and chemical testing. These tests found a portion of one of these lines, line 1107, in which general internal corrosion and localized pitting had reduced the pipe wall thickness by approximately 42 percent. Corrosion product samples taken from this line were analyzed and found to contain high levels of acid-producing bacteria. Remedial actions were completed before the affected pipelines were returned to service. On December 4, 2002, the pressure restrictions imposed by the OPS corrective action order for lines 1100, 1103, and 1110 were lifted.

After the accident, El Paso Corporation implemented an integrity management program applicable to the company's 46,000 miles of gas pipelines. An executive-level committee was formed to provide program oversight, and a company-wide pipeline integrity committee was created to directly supervise and administer the integrity management program. The internal corrosion portion of this program includes a system-wide evaluation of flow velocities, low spots in pipelines, drips, vessels, gas quality history, and liquid analysis and other operating and maintenance history and specifies follow-up remedial action. Other components of the program include operational audits, the implementation of continuous improvement processes focused on sharing best practices, enhanced communication, and the incorporation of performance metrics. In addition, the program includes in-line inspection, before 2011, of all onshore pipelines 6-inch-diameter and larger (10,551 miles for EPNG and 42,083 miles total for all pipelines operated by El Paso Corporation).

Federal Response

On August 23, 2000, RSPA issued a corrective action order (appendix B) to El Paso Energy Pipeline Group requiring EPNG to take the necessary corrective actions to protect the public and environment from potential hazards associated with its pipeline operations. The corrective action order listed 25 required corrective action items.

On August 29, 2000, RSPA issued Advisory Bulletin ADB-00-02 (appendix C) to all operators of natural gas transmission pipelines. This bulletin advised pipeline operators to review their internal corrosion monitoring programs and operations and provided guidance for doing so.

On June 20, 2001, the OPS issued to El Paso Energy Pipeline Group a notice of probable violation, proposed civil penalty, and proposed compliance order. In the notice, the OPS stated that preliminary findings indicate that internal corrosion likely played a major role in the accident. These findings also indicate that internal corrosion had probably occurred, over a long period, where liquids had accumulated in a low point in the pipeline.

The five violations alleged in the OPS notice are summarized as follows:

1. EPNG's corrosion control procedure No. 700 for pipelines 1100, 1103, and 1110 is not carried out by, or under the direction of, a person qualified in pipeline corrosion control methods. This is because EPNG's corrosion personnel have not received the informal or formal training necessary to perform the tasks required to implement the corrosion control procedures.

2. EPNG did not take steps to investigate and to minimize internal corrosion, as required by 49 CFR 192.475. EPNG failed to follow its procedures when it failed to determine that the gas transported in its pipelines was corrosive. Includes 1– Gas Control failed to recognize when water vapor levels of gas entering the pipeline exceeded Company limits and failed to stop the flow of gas into lines 1110 and 1103, 2 – Operations personnel failed to communicate with Corrosion personnel about excessive water vapor and liquid water in lines 1103 and 1110, 3 – Personnel failed to follow procedures to investigate and take corrective actions when the water vapor limits were exceeded in line 1103 and 1110, and 4 – Personnel failed to follow procedures and sound engineering practice by not performing corrosiveness tests on the liquids and solids that were removed from lines 1103 and 1110 after pigging operations.

3. EPNG did not follow its procedures for continuing surveillance by failing to consider and take appropriate action on several unusual operating and maintenance conditions on line 1103. EPNG failed to test pigging residue for corrosivity and failed to evaluate line 1103 for low points where liquids could accumulate and where corrosion could occur.

4. EPNG did not follow its Leak and Failure Reporting procedure by not following up on the Company's recommendations developed after the Roswell failure (caused by internal corrosion) and thus not minimizing the likelihood of a recurrence.

5. EPNG did not have an updated drawing of line 1103 because it did not show the elevation profile of the pipeline in the area of the accident. Having an accurate profile would have allowed EPNG to determine where low points, and possible liquid accumulation and internal corrosion, were located.

The notice proposed a civil penalty of $2.525 million for probable safety violations. On October 12, 2001, EPNG submitted a detailed response to the notice that addressed each alleged violation and requested a hearing as set forth in RSPA regulations. As of January 3, 2003, a hearing date had not been set, and a final order had not been issued.

Pipeline Integrity Management—Federal Regulations

In 1987, as the result of two gas pipeline accidents[28] that killed five persons, the Safety Board made the following safety recommendations to RSPA:

P-87-4

Require operators of both gas and liquid transmission pipelines to periodically determine the adequacy of their pipelines to operate at established maximum allowable pressures by performing inspections or tests capable of identifying corrosion-caused and other time-dependent damages that may be detrimental to the continued safe operation of these pipelines and require necessary remedial action.

P-87-5

Establish criteria for use by operators of pipelines in determining the frequency for performing inspections and tests conducted to determine the appropriateness of established maximum allowable operating pressures.

RSPA most recently responded in April 2002, stating that RSPA now requires integrity management programs for hazardous liquid pipelines in high-consequence areas, and that it (1) published a notice in the *Federal Register* on June 27, 2001, requesting comments on integrity management concepts for gas transmission pipelines, (2) published a proposed definition of high-consequence areas for gas pipelines on January 9, 2002, and (3) would propose a gas pipeline integrity management program later in 2002. On the basis of this information, Safety Recommendations P-87-4 and -5 were classified "Open—Acceptable Response" pending completion of these actions.

In 1987, as the result of a gasoline pipeline accident[29] in which two persons were killed and one person was seriously burned, the Safety Board made the following safety recommendation to RSPA:

P-87-23

Revise 49 CFR parts 192 and 195 to include operational based criteria for determining safe service intervals for pipelines between hydrostatic retests.

RSPA most recently responded in an October 11, 2002, letter summarizing the actions the agency has taken regarding pipeline integrity since the recommendation was issued. The agency told the Safety Board that over a number of years it had developed new

---

[28] National Transportation Safety Board, *Texas Eastern Gas Pipeline Company Ruptures and Fires at Beaumont, Kentucky, on April 27, 1985, and Lancaster, Kentucky, on February 21, 1986*. Pipeline Accident Report NTSB/ PAR-87-01 (Washington, D.C.; NTSB, 1987).

[29] National Transportation Safety Board, *Williams Pipe Line Company Liquid Pipeline Rupture and Fire, Mounds Views, Minnesota, July 8, 1986*. Pipeline Accident Report NTSB/PAR-87/02 (Washington, D.C.; NTSB, 1987).

approaches and had studied a number of developing technologies that are helping industry to better assess the operation of their pipelines. In addition, the letter stated that RSPA had developed a series of rulemakings that will require every natural gas transmission and hazardous liquid pipeline operator to implement an integrity management program to protect high-consequence areas that could be affected by a pipeline failure. Based on this information and information contained in an earlier (July 2002) response to this recommendation, the Safety Board classified Safety Recommendation P-87-23 "Open—Acceptable Response,"[30] pending completion of the rulemaking.

Effective September 5, 2002, RSPA issued a final rule ("Pipeline Safety: High Consequence Areas for Gas Transmission Pipelines") in which it defined "high-consequence area" as an area within a certain distance of a gas transmission pipeline that meet one or more specified criteria for the number of persons or types of property that might be affected by an accident involving that pipeline.

On December 17, 2002, the President signed Public Law 107-355, the Pipeline Safety Improvement Act of 2002. Section 14 of this act requires that within 12 months of its enactment, RSPA is to issue a final rule prescribing integrity management standards for operators of gas transmission pipelines in high-consequence areas. The act requires that within 24 months of its enactment, gas pipeline operators implement integrity management programs, even if RPSA has not issued a final rule. The act requires these pipeline operators to complete integrity testing of 50 percent of the highest risk pipelines within 5 years and the remainder within 10 years. Reassessment intervals are set at a minimum of once every 7 years. Integrity testing must be done by in-line inspection, pressure-testing, or an alternative method approved by RSPA as providing at least an equal level of safety. Under certain conditions, RSPA may grant waivers. The act requires the integrity programs to have clearly defined criteria for evaluating the results of the testing in addition to a description of actions to be taken by operators to promptly address any integrity issues raised by the evaluation.

On January 28, 2003, RSPA published in the *Federal Register* a notice of proposed rulemaking (NPRM) to require operators of gas transmission pipelines to establish integrity management programs to identify and evaluate the condition of and threats to their pipelines in high-consequence areas and to take steps to protect against pipeline failures. The proposed rule would require these pipeline operators to use periodic in-line inspections, pressure-testing, direct assessment,[31] or other means to identify weaknesses in the pipe wall. Further, the rule would require operators to gather and evaluate data on the performance trends resulting from their programs and to make improvements and corrections based on this evaluation. The rule will not apply to gas gathering or to gas distribution lines. The proposed rule would also incorporate the required elements for gas

---

[30] Safety Recommendation P-87-23 had previously been classified "Open—Unacceptable Response."

[31] *Direct assessment* is an integrity assessment method that uses a process to evaluate the threats to pipeline integrity from external corrosion, internal corrosion, and stress corrosion cracking. The process includes the gathering and integration of risk factor data, indirect examination or analysis to identify areas of suspected corrosion, direct examination of the pipeline in these areas, and post-assessment evaluation.

pipeline integrity management programs that are mandated in the Pipeline Safety Improvement Act.

NACE Standards

NACE International, an organization concerned with corrosion issues, produces consensus industry standards in the form of test methods, recommended practices, and material requirements. In 1975, the organization issued a standard, RP0175-75, "Control of Internal Corrosion in Steel Pipelines and Piping Systems." The purpose of this standard was to describe procedures and recommended practices for achieving effective control of internal corrosion in steel pipe and piping systems in crude oil, refined products, and gas service. RP0175-75 addressed methods for detecting and controlling internal corrosion and noted the importance of flow velocity analysis, periodic product sampling, and chemical analysis of corrosive constituents in mitigating corrosion. It also identified the beneficial effects of the use of cleaning pigs.

RP0175-75 was intended to serve as a guide for establishing minimum requirements for control of internal corrosion in gas transmission, gas distribution, and other steel piping systems. Because the document had not been reviewed and renewed by NACE when it was due for periodic review, in 1995 the document was withdrawn and is available from NACE only as a historical document. NACE does not consider RP0175-75 to be an official and current NACE document. The Safety Board has been told by NACE representatives that the society is working on another standard similar to, and based on, RP0175-75.

ASME Code for Gas Piping (B31.8)[32]

The American Society of Mechanical Engineers (ASME) code for gas piping addresses the safety aspects of the design, construction, operation, and maintenance of gas pipelines. Specific guidance for an internal corrosion control program for all existing pipelines is included. For pipelines that transport corrosive gas, design and construction considerations for new pipelines and modifications to existing pipelines are included. For design and construction, the considerations include (1) running cleaning pigs (including provisions for effective accumulation and handling of liquids and solids removed from the pipeline by the pigging), (2) installing corrosion monitoring devices (coupons, probes) at locations where the greatest potential for corrosion exists, (3) treating the gas to reduce its corrosivity, (4) selecting corrosion resistant materials for construction of the pipeline, (5) internally coating the pipeline, and (6) injecting corrosion inhibitors into the gas stream.

---

[32] *ASME B31.8-1999, Gas Transmission and Distribution Piping Systems*, American Society of Mechanical Engineers; Chapter VI, paragraph 863. (Essentially identical wording has been part of ASME B31.8 since 1982.) On January 31, 2002, ASME issued a supplement to the B31.8 code entitled "Managing System Integrity of Gas Pipelines," which includes guidance for determining whether internal corrosion may be a threat to pipeline integrity and measures to assess the condition of the pipeline at those locations.

For operations and maintenance, the considerations include (1) establishing a program for the detection, prevention, or mitigation of internal corrosion (including reviewing leak and repair records, inspecting the internal surface of the pipe whenever it becomes accessible, analyzing gas from areas of known internal corrosion to determine the types and concentrations of corrosive agents, analyzing liquids and solids removed from the pipeline by pigging, and draining or cleanup to determine the presence of corrosive materials and evidence of corrosion products), (2) controlling corrosion by modifying the pipeline to facilitate the removal of water from low spots, and (3) measuring the wall thickness of buried pipe when it is uncovered and of exposed pipe in areas where internal corrosion is suspected.

Guide for Gas Transmission and Distribution Piping Systems[33]

The Gas Piping Technology Committee's[34] *Guide for Gas Transmission and Distribution Piping Systems* includes material intended to assist the user in complying with the Federal regulations.[35] For internal corrosion, guidelines for design, detection, monitoring, and corrective measures are included. The guide states that in the presence of water, gases containing certain components such as CO_2, $H2_S$, and O_2 can be corrosive to steel pipelines and that pipeline liquids may contain constituents that may be detrimental to pipeline integrity. The guide also states that if it is anticipated or has been determined that the gas to be transported is corrosive, the following should be considered: selection of special materials of construction, effect of flow velocities, fluid removal (pigging, drips that include access ports for internal inspection, separators), control of water dew point (by dehydration, separation, or temperature control), reduction of corrosive components in the gas, internal coating, and chemical treatments. For the detection of internal corrosion, considerations include sampling and analysis of gas, liquids, and solids; visual inspection of pipe and drips; use of corrosion monitoring devices (coupons, probes); and in-line inspection and other non-destructive inspection to determine wall thickness.

Other Information

Previous EPNG Internal Corrosion Accident

On September 10, 1996, line 1300 ruptured near Roswell, New Mexico. The EPNG investigation determined that the pipe had failed from internal corrosion at a sag bend in the pipe. The accident report stated that:

---

[33] ANSI GPTC Z380.1, *Guide for Gas Transmission and Distribution Piping Systems,* Gas Piping Technology Committee.

[34] The Gas Piping Technology Committee is an independent consensus committee comprising representatives from the pipeline industry, including manufacturers, operators, and consultants, as well as from pipeline regulatory agencies.

[35] The current guide is dated June 15, 1998, and includes Addendum No. 1, July 7, 1999; Addendum No. 2, August 23, 2000; and Addendum No. 3, January 29, 2002. The guide material for internal corrosion was most recently revised in Addendum 3.

it is impossible to tell when in time most of the corrosion at the rupture point occurred. However, it is certainly related to the settlement of liquids in a low spot, possibly during the period of low flows in the line for several years prior to its reversal in 1992. The source of liquids was probably one or more of the production facilities that provide (or provided) gas directly to the transmission line. Current analyses do not provide adequate information to determine the presence of potentially corrosive liquids in gas received, so other measures should be taken to prevent the introduction of liquids into the line.

The metallurgy report, which was an attachment to EPNG's final investigation report of the rupture, recommended that the quality of gas being injected into line 1300 near the rupture location and at other locations of concern be monitored to avoid another failure of this type. Also recommended were (1) that pigs be run near the failure location to clean any remaining liquid from the system, (2) that a sample of the pigging residue be analyzed to determine whether undesirable compounds were present, (3) that other areas of possible pipeline deflection be examined, and (4) that previously untested areas in the vicinity of the rupture be hydrostatically tested to ensure their structural integrity.

In a Safety Board interview, a member of the EPNG pipeline safety staff stated that the company considered the failure of line 1300 to be an isolated event and that the recommendations in the investigation report were therefore applicable only to line 1300 because of unique operating conditions in the ruptured pipeline. These conditions included a producer that EPNG representatives said had been known to introduce water into the pipeline at a receipt point near the rupture location, as well as periods of low-flow and static conditions in line 1300, which resulted in gas flow rates insufficient to move or dissipate the moisture.

Emergency Training and Simulations

Annual meetings of emergency responders were conducted in November 1997, October 1998, October 1999, and October 2000 for the Carlsbad area, including Eddy County, emergency response and law enforcement agencies. At these meetings, EPNG personnel reiterated safety precautions at natural gas emergencies and, through written tests, quizzed emergency responders on safety issues.

In November 1997, EPNG conducted an emergency response exercise for a leak on line 3191 between South Carlsbad compressor station and Pecos River compressor station. The Eddy County Sheriff's Office was involved, as well as the Eddy County disaster coordinator. In August 1997, a leak was simulated at the Keystone compressor station to test the readiness of the compressor station personnel.

Analysis

EPNG pipeline 1103 was operating at about 80 percent of the maximum allowable operating pressure when the pipeline ruptured. The rupture occurred at a place in the pipeline where internal corrosion had thinned the pipe wall. The fact that the fracture faces resulted from overstress separation with no evidence of fatigue cracking indicates that the rupture occurred as one catastrophic event. The Safety Board therefore concludes that line 1103 ruptured as a result of severe internal corrosion that caused a reduction in pipe wall thickness to the point that the remaining metal could no longer contain the pressure within the pipe.

A number of factors were found to have contributed to the fact that the corrosion that led to the rupture had not been detected and mitigated by EPNG before the accident, and those factors are addressed in this analysis.

The major safety issues identified during the investigation of this accident are as follows:

- The design and construction of the pipeline,

- The adequacy of EPNG's internal corrosion control program,

- The adequacy of Federal safety regulations for gas pipelines, and

- The adequacy of Federal oversight of the pipeline operator.

Exclusions

The investigation determined that the operating pressure (675 psig) in the pipeline at the time of the rupture was below the maximum allowable operating pressure (837 psig) established for that section of the pipeline. Operation of the pipeline system was monitored by a SCADA system, and even though the gas controller's understanding of the rapidly unfolding situation at the Pecos River compressor station immediately after the rupture was hampered by a brief interruption of data from the SCADA system and the subsequent loss of SCADA communications as a result of the power outage at the Pecos River compressor station, the controller accurately evaluated the available information and promptly initiated an appropriate response. There was no evidence of third-party damage to the pipeline at the rupture site, nor was there evidence of external corrosion at the rupture location. The Safety Board therefore concludes that the following were neither causal nor contributory to the accident or its aftermath: overpressure of the pipeline, the interruption in or loss of SCADA communication, external damage to the pipeline through excavation or other activities, and external corrosion of the pipeline.

Emergency Response

EPNG employees, who were on the accident scene within 19 minutes of the rupture, worked quickly and effectively to stop the flow of natural gas from the ruptured pipeline and to extinguish the fire. Because they did not know which pipeline had ruptured, they began closing valves upstream and downstream of the fireball in all four EPNG natural gas pipelines. Emergency responders arrived on scene within 25 minutes of the rupture and staged at the Pecos River compressor station. The emergency responders anticipated a routine standby assignment that would terminate when the flow of natural gas was stopped and the fire self-extinguished. Because the accident was in a rural area, emergency responders did not expect to find any persons injured. However, approximately 40 minutes after the rupture and while attempting to reach valves to stop the flow of natural gas, an EPNG employee thought that he saw vehicles in the area of the fire and provided that information to another employee.

About 15 minutes later, when the flow of natural gas was stopped and the fire was extinguished, the EPNG employee confirmed that he had seen vehicles in the area where the fire had been burning. This information was then passed on to emergency responders, who immediately initiated rescue efforts. Carlsbad Fire Department's medic units had responded with the initial call and were staged at the compressor station. Paramedics and emergency medical technicians worked diligently to treat the injuries of victims and to hastily evacuate them to hospital burn centers in Texas.

The Safety Board notes that the EPNG employees who initially had information that vehicles may be parked in the vicinity of the fire did not notify emergency responders until the fire was extinguished and the presence of vehicles was confirmed. In order for emergency responders to make informed decisions about rescue efforts, it is important that they be given information, as quickly as it is available, that could indicate the possibility of victims in the vicinity of an accident. In this case, because of the intensity of the fire in the vicinity of the campsite, the radiant heat associated with the fire, and the difficulty that response crews would have faced gaining access to the area while the fire was burning, the Safety Board does not believe the outcome of the accident would have been different if responders had been notified sooner, although the precise effect such notification would have had on responders' decision-making cannot be determined.

Internal Corrosion in Steel Gas Pipelines

Corrosion on the internal wall of a natural gas pipeline can occur when the pipe wall is exposed to water and contaminants in the gas, such as O_2, H_2S, CO_2, or chlorides. The nature and extent of the corrosion damage that may occur are functions of the concentration and particular combinations of these various corrosive constituents within the pipe, as well as of the operating conditions of the pipeline. For example, gas velocity and temperature in the pipeline play a significant role in determining if and where corrosion damage may occur. In other words, a particular gas composition may cause corrosion under some operating conditions but not others. Therefore, it would be difficult to develop a precise definition of the term "corrosive gas" that would be universally applicable under all operating conditions.

Corrosion may also be caused or facilitated by the activity of microorganisms living on the pipe wall. Referred to as microbiologically influenced corrosion, or MIC, this type of corrosion can occur when microbes and nutrients are available and where water, corrosion products, deposits, etc., present on the pipe wall provide sites favorable for the colonization of microbes. Microbial activity, in turn, may create concentration cells or produce organic acids or acid-producing gases, making the environment aggressive for carbon steel. The microbes can also metabolize sulfur or sulfur compounds to produce products that are corrosive to steel or that otherwise accelerate the attack on steel.

Internal corrosion in a gas pipeline may be detected by any of several methods, including visual examination of the inside of a pipeline when it is opened, external measurement of the pipe wall thickness with instruments, evaluation of corrosion coupons or probes placed inside the pipeline, or inspection of the pipe with an in-line inspection tool to identify areas of pitting or metal loss.

Internal corrosion may be kept under control by establishing appropriate pipeline operating conditions and by using corrosion-mitigation techniques. One method for reducing the potential for internal corrosion to occur is to control the quality of gas entering the pipeline. Also, by periodically sampling and analyzing the gas, liquids, and solids removed from the pipeline to detect the presence and concentration of any corrosive contaminants, including bacteria, as well as to detect evidence of corrosion products, a pipeline operator can determine if detrimental corrosion may be occurring, identify the cause(s) of the corrosion, and develop corrosion control measures.

Internal Corrosion in Line 1103

Interconnecting pits were observed on the inside of the pipe in the ruptured area of line 1103. Typically, these pits showed the striations and undercutting features that are often associated with microbial corrosion. A pit profile showed that chloride concentration in the pits increased steadily from top to bottom. Increased chloride concentration can result from certain types of microbial activity. All four types of microbes (sulfate-reducing, acid-producing, general aerobic, and anaerobic) were observed in samples collected from two pit areas in the piece of line 1103 where internal corrosion was discovered after the accident about 2,080 feet downstream of the rupture site. Though the individual contribution of various microbes in the corrosion process could not be estimated, the damage morphology and the corrosion product analyses data suggest that microbiological activity contributed to the corrosion process.

Dissolved O_2 in an electrolyte could cause pitting by creating concentration cells. CO_2 is soluble in water and will form carbonic acid, which is corrosive to carbon steel.

When dissolved in water, H_2S forms a weak acid that could corrode carbon steel. In combination with dissolved O_2, it could cause pitting. Though generally present in low concentrations, these potentially corrosive constituents were present in the gas that was being transported in line 1103. Also, upset conditions occasionally increased the concentrations of these constituents in the transported gas.

Chlorides were observed in all corrosion product/deposit samples. Anions, such as chloride, cause pitting and, typically, chloride concentration in a pit may be much higher than the chloride concentration outside the pit (bulk concentration).

Chemical analyses showed that the pH (6.7-6.8) of the liquid collected at the Pecos River compressor station plant inlet separator scrubber was more acidic than the pH (8.2) of the liquid collected at Keystone compressor station inlet scrubber. Also, the material collected at line 1100 and 1103 pig receivers (pH ~ 6.2-6.3) and the inside material collected from a low spot on line 1103 west of the rupture (pH ~ 6.4) were more acidic than the material collected near the siphon drain area of the line 1103 drip (pH ~ 8.9). The observed low pH in the samples could be a result of dissolved CO_2, and/or H_2S in the water, and/or intrusion of low-pH ground water into the gas supply. Typically, acidic (pH<7) water is more corrosive to carbon steel than basic water (pH>7).

Thus, water and contaminants such as chlorides, O_2 CO_2, and H_2S all likely contributed to the observed corrosion damage. The Safety Board therefore concludes that the corrosion that was found in line 1103 at the rupture site was likely caused by a combination within the pipeline of microbes and such contaminants as moisture, chlorides, O_2, CO_2, and H_2S.

Physical Features of Line 1103

Examination of the pipe at the rupture location revealed five wrinkles in the pipe wall at the top of the pipeline. Wrinkles in the wall of a pipe occur when a pipe is bent, either to align pieces of pipe during construction or from external forces, such as earth movement, after the pipeline is in service. When pipe is bent and wrinkles form on the top of the pipe, a low point is created at the bottom of the pipe opposite the wrinkles. The observed internal corrosion in the pipeline at the rupture location was at such a low point, where liquids likely accumulated into a pool with a fluctuating liquid level. Because the density of water is greater than that of hydrocarbon liquids present in the pipeline, water in the pipeline would remain at the bottom of the pool with the liquid hydrocarbons on top, creating an ideal environment for the development of internal corrosion.

The original construction of line 1103 by EPNG included a block valve and drip approximately 1 mile east of the Pecos River. The block valve, designated No. 6, was on a hill about 62 feet higher than the Pecos River. The valve may have been positioned thus so that it would remain accessible and not be damaged if the river flooded. The underground drip was placed downstream of the block valve and was 31 feet lower in elevation than the pipeline at block valve No. 6. This configuration facilitated the trapping of liquids and solids flowing in line 1103 toward the Pecos River compressor station by the drip, which was upstream of the rupture location.

When pigging facilities were added to line 1103 about 25 years after initial construction, a pig launcher was installed at block valve No. 2, and a pig receiver was placed at block valve No. 6. A separate storage leg or tank to collect the pig liquids at block valve No. 6 was not installed. Instead, during pigging operations, the pig and some of the liquids and solids being pushed by the pig would be caught in the pig receiver at block valve No. 6. Any material that passed the pig receiver, either during normal operations or because of a pig run, would flow downstream and downhill to the drip.

Postaccident visual examination of the drip revealed that, at one point, about 70 percent of the drip cross-section was filled with the blackish oily-powdery/grainy material that acted as a dam inside the drip, preventing some of the materials entering the drip from continuing to the far end of the barrel to the siphon drain. This blockage also likely contributed to movement of liquids and solids past the drip. Materials flowing past the drip could then collect at low points in the downstream pipeline, such as the low point at the rupture location, where they would remain until gas flow of sufficient velocity was available to sweep the liquids farther downstream toward the inlet scrubbers at the Pecos River compressor station. Velocity data provided by EPNG for the period 1991 to 2000 indicated numerous periods when the gas velocity was substantially below the preferred sweeping velocity of 25 feet per second.

The Safety Board concludes that, as a likely result of the partial clogging of the drip upstream of the rupture location, some liquids bypassed the drip, continued through the pipeline, and accumulated and caused corrosion at the eventual rupture site where pipe bending had created a low point in the pipeline.

Periodic use of cleaning pigs can remove water and other liquid and solid contaminants from a pipeline. One of the considerations for the design and construction of a cleaning pig system is to make provisions for effective collection and removal of the accumulated materials from the pipeline after pigging. In line 1103, because of the configuration of the piping and valves at block valve No. 6 and the geometry of the drip, cleaning pigs could not be run in the section of pipeline that ruptured. Some of the liquids and solids that accumulated in front of the cleaning pig were returned to the pipeline and moved downstream by the flowing gas toward the drip. In conjunction with the partially clogged drip, and the introduction of additional liquids into line 1103 from the crossover from line 1100 (from which the drip had been removed) upstream of the line 1103 drip, it is likely that there was incomplete removal of accumulated liquids and solids from line 1103.

Postaccident in-line inspection of the segment of line 1103 in which cleaning pigs had been periodically run (from block valve No. 2 to block valve No. 6) found no areas of internal corrosion that the company determined required repair. The Safety Board therefore concludes that if the accident section of pipeline 1103 had been able to accommodate cleaning pigs, and if cleaning pigs had been used regularly with the resulting liquids and solids thoroughly removed from the pipeline after each pig run, the internal corrosion that developed in this section of pipe would likely have been less severe.

The ASME code for gas piping (ASME B31.8, *Gas Transmission and Distribution Piping Systems*) and the *Guide for Gas Transmission and Distribution Piping Systems* include design and construction considerations related to internal corrosion control for new pipelines and modifications to existing pipelines. Although some operators may incorporate these considerations or have their own engineering standards for the design and construction of pipelines to minimize liquid accumulation and to remove liquids from a pipeline, there are no Federal regulatory requirements applicable to all operators.

The Safety Board believes that RSPA should revise 49 CFR Part 192 to require that new or replaced pipelines be designed and constructed with features to mitigate internal corrosion. At a minimum, such pipelines should (1) be configured to minimize the accumulation of liquids, (2) be equipped with effective liquid removal features, and (3) be able to accommodate corrosion monitoring devices at locations with the greatest potential for internal corrosion.

EPNG Internal Corrosion Control Program

At the time of the accident, EPNG was beginning the process of implementing an internal corrosion control program based on the new procedures dated May 15, 2000, and July 10, 2000. However, training of personnel in the new procedures began in August 2000, and the new corrosion control actions specified in these documents had yet to be fully implemented at the time of the accident. As a result, the program actually in place was the one specified in the September 20, 1999, operating and maintenance procedures manual. This written program required (1) that the corrosion services department, after being notified that corrosive gas was being transported or if internal corrosion was found, recommend appropriate corrective actions and establish an internal corrosion monitoring program to determine the effectiveness of the corrective actions, and (2) that a visual inspection he made of the inside of a pipeline when opened.

These procedures did not address the specific operating conditions, such as water in the pipeline, corrosive contaminants in the gas and liquid, and velocity of the gas, that should be considered when evaluating a pipeline for possible internal corrosion. The company's gas quality standard addressed several contaminants, including water, CO_2, H_2S, and O_2, but the corrosion control procedures did not reference these contaminants or their acceptable limits. Although gas quality standards were contained in EPNG's contracts with gas suppliers, most of the interconnect locations with gas producers on line 1103 (between the Pecos River compressor station and the Keystone compressor station) and line 1100 (between Eunice plant and the Keystone compressor station, from which gas and liquids could enter line 1103 upstream of the drip) did not have alarms (which alarmed in the gas control center if contaminant levels were exceeded), and other locations only had periodic sampling and analysis of the gas entering the EPNG pipeline. Thus, despite the fact that EPNG officials said they relied partially on maintaining the quality of gas to help prevent corrosion, the company did not take the steps necessary to allow it to adequately monitor and control the quality of gas entering the pipeline.

The 1999 procedures did not provide guidance regarding how internal corrosion would be detected other than through visual inspection of a pipe segment after it had been opened. Nor did the procedures require that, during normal operations, pigging, or maintenance activities, liquids and solids be removed from the pipeline and tested for the presence of corrosive materials or evidence of corrosion products. The ASME B31.8 code identifies the importance of determining whether gas is corrosive by requiring that "Gas containing free water under the conditions at which it will be transported shall be assumed to be corrosive, unless proven to be non-corrosive by recognized tests or experience." Very little useful information concerning what was entering the pipeline, where it was entering, and what materials were accumulating in the pipeline was available to corrosion control personnel. As a result, EPNG corrosion control personnel stated that they were not aware that corrosion could be occurring in the company's pipeline or that corrosion mitigation measures might be necessary.

In the event it was determined that corrosive gas was being transported or internal corrosion was occurring, corrosion mitigation actions would be recommended by the corrosion services department. However, there were no written requirements for corrosion technicians to follow up on reports of out-of-specification gas being received or to identify the effect, if any, of this gas on the pipeline, and there were no standards or criteria to be used to determine if out-of-specification gas was potentially corrosive. The procedures did not detail how the semi-annual monitoring to determine the effectiveness of the corrosion mitigation measures would be carried out. Corrosion monitoring devices were not used in line 1103 between the Keystone and Pecos River stations because the gas was not believed to be corrosive.

In September 1996, EPNG's line 1300 ruptured as a result of internal corrosion. The metallurgy report attached to EPNG's final investigation report of the rupture recommended expanded gas quality monitoring and additional pigging, with collected residue being analyzed for undesirable components. Because the company considered this rupture to be an isolated event, it did not implement the recommendations for its other, similar, gas transmission lines. Further, according to a senior safety staff employee at EPNG, the company's internal audit program was not revised after the September 1996 rupture of line 1300 from internal corrosion. Revising the company's audit program to include inquiries regarding operating conditions (gas velocity, gas producers connected to a transmission pipeline, unpigged pipelines whose configuration could lead to accumulation of liquids in low spots) would have helped EPNG to determine if similar conditions existed in other pipelines, but the company did not do so.

In the years leading up to the accident, EPNG had access to industry standards and guidelines, such as those contained in the NACE standards, the ASME code, and the *Guide for Gas Transmission and Distribution Piping Systems*, regarding the detection and control of internal pipeline corrosion. But the company did not incorporate that guidance in its internal corrosion procedures. Nor did the company take the steps necessary to ensure that the limited procedures that it did have in place were effective. For example, while the procedures in place at the time of the accident stated that corrosion control personnel were to be notified if corrosive gas was being transported, the company did not, as noted above, carry out the gas quality monitoring or inspection activities necessary to make an accurate determination of the corrosivity of the gas. Also, the procedures required that corrosion control personnel be notified if corrosion was found, but the company had no systematic program to detect possible internal corrosion. Internal inspection devices or corrosion coupons that could have detected existing or potential corrosion were not regularly employed. In the view of the Safety Board, the preaccident approach of EPNG in regard to internal corrosion indicates that the company did not believe internal corrosion to be a significant issue in the safety of its pipeline operations. As a result, the company was inadequately attentive to the potential for severe internal corrosion to occur, with the result that the corrosion that led to the rupture of line 1103 was not detected and mitigated in time to prevent a serious accident. The Safety Board therefore concludes that, before the accident, EPNG did not have in place an internal corrosion control program that was adequate to identify or mitigate the internal corrosion that was occurring in its pipelines.

After the acquisition of Sonat in January 2000, which had been preceded by the acquisition of Tenneco Energy in December 1996, El Paso Energy organized teams of representatives from each pipeline to determine best practices and produce a new operating and maintenance manual. The resulting *Operating and Maintenance Procedures* manual was issued on May 15, 2000, followed by a *Corrosion Control Manual* on July 10, 2000. These procedures were applicable to El Paso Energy's gas pipeline companies and were the approved procedures at the time of the accident in August 2000.

For Tenneco Energy, the internal corrosion procedures in use at the time of the December 1996 acquisition by EPNG were in the company's *Operating and Maintenance Manual*. The procedure for internal corrosion detection and control was dated December 1, 1993, and included a requirement to test gas and liquids being transported to determine if they are corrosive. A *Corrosion Control Manual* dated February 1, 1997 supplemented the internal corrosion control procedures in the *Operating and Maintenance Manual* with additional, detailed internal corrosion control considerations and measures.

Even though EPNG had access to Tenneco's procedures after the acquisition, it took an additional 41 months, from December 1996 to May 2000, for El Paso Energy to develop and issue internal corrosion control procedures applicable to EPNG that included requirements for testing pipeline gas and liquids to determine if they are corrosive. It was an additional 2 months, from May 15 to July 10, 2000, before the supplemental, detailed internal corrosion control procedures were issued describing what to test for, where to test, and how often to test.

The program being implemented at the time of the accident was based on EPNG's *Corrosion Control Manual,* Section 700, dated July 10, 2000 (subsequently revised January 15, 2001, revised October 1, 2001, and redesignated Section 6 and revised December 19, 2001). The program recognized that gas quality standards alone are insufficient to determine whether a pipeline is transporting corrosive gas. These procedures state that the first line of defense against internal corrosion is gas and liquid quality standards but that whether a pipeline transports corrosive gas cannot be determined from the standards themselves. Also noted in the documents is that industry experience has shown that water and other corrosives may enter the pipeline by accident or by operational upsets or that it may slowly accumulate in low spots despite gas quality monitoring that shows adherence to quality standards. The procedures state that "identification of corrosive gas in a pipeline is achieved by analysis of operating conditions, gas impurity content, monitoring data, mitigation schemes, and/or other considerations" and that "an effective internal corrosion-monitoring program includes sampling and analysis of liquid, gas, and solid materials." After the accident, the Safety Board's analysis of the liquids and solids from the pipeline determined that potentially corrosive constituents such as water, chlorides, and bacteria were present in the pipeline. The Safety Board concludes that had EPNG effectively monitored the quality of gas entering the pipeline and the operating conditions in pipeline 1103 and periodically sampled and analyzed the liquids and solids that were removed from the line, it would likely have determined that the potential existed for significant corrosion to occur within the pipeline.

Federal Safety Regulations

Federal regulations for gas pipelines include two sections that have requirements for an internal corrosion control program and one section that requires that the procedures for the program be included in the operator's operating and maintenance manual. The regulations do not define "corrosive gas" but do state that such gas may not be transported by pipeline unless its effect on the pipeline has been investigated and steps have been taken to minimize internal corrosion. For internal corrosion to occur, water must typically be present in the pipeline, along with corrosive contaminants such as chlorides, H_2S, CO_2, O_2, or bacteria. The regulations do not specifically address microbiologically influenced corrosion or the way that water and contaminants in the pipeline can combine to contribute to the corrosion process. The regulations also do not specifically address the importance of the following: minimizing liquids and liquid accumulation in the pipeline, removing liquids from the pipeline, maintaining drips, and the role of gas velocity in corrosion control.

Because the Federal regulations do not specifically address the above issues, the Safety Board concludes that the current Federal pipeline safety regulations do not provide adequate guidance to pipeline operators or enforcement personnel in mitigating pipeline internal corrosion. The Safety Board therefore believes that RSPA should develop the requirements necessary to ensure that pipeline operators' internal corrosion control programs address the role of water and other contaminants in the corrosion process.

Federal Oversight of the Pipeline Operator

On May 15, 2000, EPNG issued revised operating and maintenance procedures for internal corrosion control. For each of the six OPS safety inspections of EPNG conducted between May 15 and September 25, 2000, compliance with the Federal regulations for internal corrosion control was noted by the inspectors as "satisfactory." After the accident, however, the OPS cited EPNG for a number of probable violations related to its internal corrosion program. For example, in its June 20, 2001, notice of probable violation, the OPS stated that EPNG's internal corrosion control program was not carried out by, or under the direction of, a person qualified in pipeline corrosion control methods. But in each of the six inspections between May 15 and September 25, 2000, OPS inspectors had noted that the company's program was "…under the direction of a qualified person, with associated records…." In several cases, the inspector included on the form a brief description of the qualifications of EPNG's principal coordinator of corrosion services. At no time did the OPS inspection process, even under the system integrity inspection pilot program, indicate a personnel qualification issue with EPNG's corrosion program.

The postaccident notice of probable violation also cited EPNG for not following its own procedures and sound engineering practice by not performing corrosiveness tests on the liquids and solids that were removed from lines 1103 and 1110 after pigging operations. But at no time during the inspections conducted before September 2000 did the OPS indicate that such testing of liquids and solids was required or that it was sound engineering practice.

In addition, the notice of probable violation stated that EPNG's elevation profile drawings for its pipelines in the area of the Pecos River were incomplete. Specifically, the notice stated that the drawings did not show any elevation profile for line 1103 between block valve No. 6 and the Pecos River compressor station. Therefore, according to the OPS, EPNG did not know the location of low points in the pipeline where liquids could accumulate and thus could not take certain corrosion control steps that could possibly have prevented the accident. However, during none of the six inspections between May and September 2000 did the OPS indicate that profile drawings of pipelines were required or that there were any other compliance or safety issues with the pipeline maps.

Further, in April 2000, the OPS conducted a team review of EPNG's operating and maintenance procedures as part of the system integrity inspection pilot program. No deficiencies in the procedures were identified in this inspection, and the OPS did not require any follow-up actions by EPNG to correct compliance and safety problems. But only four questions related to an internal corrosion control program (coupon monitoring and records and corrosion remedial measures and records) were included on the inspection form. The inspection form did not inquire into the four components of an effective internal corrosion control program identified in the regulations (determining whether corrosive gas is being transported, inspection of pipe removed from a pipeline, qualification of internal corrosion control personnel, and qualification of the person directing the internal corrosion control program). Thus, because its inspections did not seek information from the operator in these four areas, the OPS did not have sufficient basis for evaluating EPNG's compliance with the Federal regulations for internal corrosion control.

Throughout the inspections conducted by the OPS to qualify EPNG for the system integrity inspection pilot program, OPS inspection reports documented that EPNG's internal audit program was working as designed. However, the procedures and forms used by EPNG for its internal audits only addressed actions to be taken after it had been determined that corrosive gas was being transported. Not addressed in either the EPNG procedures or forms reviewed by the OPS was how to determine if corrosive gas was being transported. Thus, although the program was functioning, the internal audit program was not adequate to uncover potential deficiencies in the company's internal corrosion control program.

Federal inspections of a pipeline operator should provide the operator with accurate feedback and the opportunity for immediate, constructive dialog with the OPS. In addition, the OPS uses data obtained during field inspections to assess the effectiveness of its regulations and identify issues of operator noncompliance. But in this case, the OPS postaccident investigation documented deficiencies in EPNG operations that it had not previously identified. Had the preaccident inspections applied the enforcement criteria in the same manner as they were interpreted after the accident, EPNG may have been prompted to correct deficiencies in its programs. The Safety Board concludes that the OPS did not make accurate preaccident assessments of EPNG's internal corrosion program and therefore did not identify deficiencies in the program before the accident. The Safety Board therefore believes that RSPA should evaluate the OPS's pipeline operator inspection program to identify deficiencies that resulted in the failure of inspectors, before the Carlsbad, New Mexico, accident, to identify the inadequacies in EPNG's internal corrosion control program. The Safety Board further believes that RSPA should implement the changes necessary to ensure adequate assessments of pipeline operator safety programs.

Industry Standards

As shown by this accident, pipeline failure due to internal corrosion can have serious consequences and, in the view of the Safety Board, industry standards and recommended practices such as NACE RP0175-75, "Control of Internal Corrosion In Steel Pipelines and Piping Systems," can be of significant benefit to pipeline operators. The Safety Board is concerned that, because RP0175-75 is not considered current and may contain outdated information, pipeline operators may not have easy access to information that could contribute significantly to the establishment of an effective internal corrosion control program. Even though the Safety Board has been told by NACE representatives that the society is working on a new standard to replace RP0175-75, no timetable has been given for the completion of this effort. The Safety Board believes that NACE International should establish an accelerated schedule for completion of an industry standard for the control of internal corrosion in steel pipelines that will replace or update NACE standard RP0175-75.

Conclusions

Findings

1. The following were neither causal nor contributory to the accident or its aftermath: overpressure of the pipeline, the interruption in or loss of supervisory control and data acquisition system communication, external damage to the pipeline through excavation or other activities, and external corrosion of the pipeline.

2. Line 1103 ruptured as a result of severe internal corrosion that caused a reduction in pipe wall thickness to the point that the remaining metal could no longer contain the pressure within the pipe.

3. The corrosion that was found in line 1103 at the rupture site was likely caused by a combination within the pipeline of microbes and such contaminants as moisture, chlorides, oxygen, carbon dioxide, and hydrogen sulfide.

4. If the accident section of pipeline 1103 had been able to accommodate cleaning pigs, and if cleaning pigs had been used regularly with the resulting liquids and solids thoroughly removed from the pipeline after each pig run, the internal corrosion that developed in this section of pipe would likely have been less severe.

5. As a likely result of the partial clogging of the "drip" upstream of the rupture location, some liquids bypassed the drip, continued through the pipeline, and accumulated and caused corrosion at the eventual rupture site where pipe bending had created a low point in the pipeline.

6. Had El Paso Natural Gas Company effectively monitored the quality of gas entering the pipeline and the operating conditions in pipeline 1103 and periodically sampled and analyzed the liquids and solids that were removed from the line, it would likely have determined that the potential existed for significant corrosion to occur within the pipeline.

7. Before the accident, El Paso Natural Gas Company did not have in place an internal corrosion control program that was adequate to identify or mitigate the internal corrosion that was occurring in its pipelines.

8. The current Federal pipeline safety regulations do not provide adequate guidance to pipeline operators or enforcement personnel in mitigating pipeline internal corrosion.

9. The Office of Pipeline Safety did not make accurate preaccident assessments of El Paso Natural Gas Company's internal corrosion control program and therefore did not identify deficiencies in the program before the accident.

Probable Cause

The National Transportation Safety Board determines that the probable cause of the August 19, 2000, natural gas pipeline rupture and subsequent fire near Carlsbad, New Mexico, was a significant reduction in pipe wall thickness due to severe internal corrosion. The severe corrosion had occurred because El Paso Natural Gas Company's corrosion control program failed to prevent, detect, or control internal corrosion within the company's pipeline. Contributing to the accident were ineffective Federal preaccident inspections of El Paso Natural Gas Company that did not identify deficiencies in the company's internal corrosion control program.

Recommendations

As a result of its investigation of the August 19, 2000, pipeline rupture and subsequent fire near Carlsbad, New Mexico, the National Transportation Safety Board makes the following safety recommendations:

To the Research and Special Programs Administration:

Revise 49 *Code of Federal Regulations* Part 192 to require that new or replaced pipelines be designed and constructed with features to mitigate internal corrosion. At a minimum, such pipelines should (1) be configured to reduce the opportunity for liquids to accumulate, (2) be equipped with effective liquid removal features, and (3) be able to accommodate corrosion monitoring devices at locations with the greatest potential for internal corrosion. (P-03-1)

Develop the requirements necessary to ensure that pipeline operators' internal corrosion control programs address the role of water and other contaminants in the corrosion process. (P-03-2)

Evaluate the Office of Pipeline Safety's pipeline operator inspection program to identify deficiencies that resulted in the failure of inspectors, before the Carlsbad, New Mexico, accident, to identify the inadequacies in El Paso Natural Gas Company's internal corrosion control program. Implement the changes necessary to ensure adequate assessments of pipeline operator safety programs. (P-03-3)

To NACE International:

Establish an accelerated schedule for completion of an industry standard for the control of internal corrosion in steel pipelines that will replace or update NACE standard RP0175-75. (P-03-4)

BY THE NATIONAL TRANSPORTATION SAFETY BOARD

JOHN A. HAMMERSCHMIDT
Acting Chairman

JOHN J. GOGLIA
Member

CAROL J. CARMODY
Member

Adopted: February 11, 2003

Appendix A

Investigation

The National Transportation Safety Board was notified on August 19, 2000, through the National Response Center, of a pipeline explosion and fire south of Carlsbad, New Mexico. The Safety Board dispatched an investigative team from its Washington, D.C., headquarters. The team comprised investigative groups in pipeline operations, corrosion, survival factors, and family assistance. Board Members John Hammerschmidt and Carol Carmody accompanied the investigative team. Then-Chairman Jim Hall was also at the accident site during the on-scene portion of the investigation. No hearings or depositions were held in conjunction with the investigation. Representatives from El Paso Natural Gas Company and the Office of Pipeline Safety participated in the investigation.

Appendix B

Summary of Office of Pipeline Safety Corrective Action Order

On August 23, 2000, the Office of Pipeline Safety issued a corrective action order requiring EPNG to take the necessary corrective actions to protect the public and environment from potential hazards associated with its pipeline operations.

The corrective action order listed 25 required corrective action items, summarized as follows:

Line 1110 between block valve No. 6 and the Pecos River compressor station:

- Utilizing x-ray and ultrasonic examination techniques, assess the integrity of the pipeline at all locations that may have a no-flow condition or where liquids may accumulate, and implement corrective actions;

- Hydrostatically test the pipeline to at least 90 percent SMYS;

- Prepare status reports and summary of findings and submit to RSPA;

- After return to service plan is approved by RSPA, restrict the operating pressure to 538 psig (80 percent of actual pressure at the time of the failure); maintain pressure restriction until released by OPS.

Line 1103 between block valve No. 6 and the Pecos River compressor station:

- Remain out of service until additional information about the rupture is reviewed.

Line 1100 between station 2482+52 (6.1 miles upstream of block valve No. 6) and the Pecos River compressor station:

- Utilizing x-ray and ultrasonic examination techniques, assess the integrity of the pipeline at all locations that may have a no-flow condition or where liquids may accumulate, and implement corrective actions;

- Obtain OPS approval for the design of the temporary crossing of the Pecos River;

- Hydrostatically test the pipeline to at least 90 percent SMYS;

- Prepare status reports and summary of findings and submit to RSPA;

- After return to service plan is approved by RSPA, restrict the operating pressure to 538 psig (80 percent of actual pressure at the time of the failure); maintain pressure restriction until released by OPS.

Lines 1103 and 1110 between Keystone Compressor Station and Guadalupe Compressor Station, and Line 1100 between Eunice plant and Gaudalupe Compressor Station:

- Restrict operating pressure to 668 psig (80 percent of MAOP) until released by RSPA;

- Develop a risk-based plan to inspect for indications of internal corrosion and assess and correct (1) areas in the pipeline that cannot be inspected with an internal inspection tool, (2) areas that may have a no-flow condition, and (3) areas where liquids may accumulate;

- Provide RSPA with an analysis of the continued safe operation of lines 1100, 1103, and 1110.

All pipelines operated by EPNG:

- Obtain OPS approval of corrective action plans, which must describe the criteria for evaluating corroded areas and the criteria used to select the corrective action;

- Complete the submission of EPNG's pipeline system information to the National Pipeline Mapping System;

- Obtain OPS approval for design of the permanent crossings of the Pecos River;

- Develop a risk-based plan to inspect for indications of internal corrosion and assess and correct (1) areas in the pipeline that cannot be inspected with an internal inspection tool, (2) areas that may have a no-flow condition, and (3) areas where liquids may accumulate.

Appendix C

Research and Special Programs Administration Advisory Bulletin

On August 29, 2000, the Research and Special Programs Administration issued Advisory Bulletin ADB-00-02 to all operators of natural gas transmission pipelines:

DEPARTMENT OF TRANSPORTATION

Research and Special Programs Administration

1. Pipeline Safety: Internal Corrosion in Gas Transmission Pipelines

AGENCY: Research and Special Programs Administration (RSPA), DOT

ACTION: Notice; issuance of advisory bulletin.

SUMMARY: The Office of Pipeline Safety (OPS) is issuing this bulletin to owners and operators of natural gas transmission pipeline systems to advise them to review their internal corrosion programs. Operators should consider factors that influence the formation of internal corrosion, including gas quality and operating parameters. Operators should give special attention to pipeline alignment features that may contribute to internal corrosion by allowing condensates to settle out of the gas stream. This action follows a review of incidents involving internal corrosion, some of which resulted in loss of life, injuries, and significant property damage. OPS' preliminary investigation of a recent gas transmission pipeline incident found wall thinning on damaged pipe associated with the incident. The wall thinning is consistent with that caused by internal corrosion.

SUPPLEMENTARY INFORMATION:

I. Background

Internal corrosion control in gas transmission pipelines is addressed in the Federal pipeline safety regulations at 49 CFR 192.475 and 192.477. Internal corrosion is most often found in gas transmission pipelines and appurtenances in the vicinity of production and gathering facilities or storage fields.

An OPS review of incident reports and inspections indicated that better industry guidance is needed to determine the best practices for monitoring the potential for internal corrosion in gas transmission pipelines. Some methods for monitoring internal corrosion are weight loss coupons, radiography, water chemistry tests, in-line inspection tools, and electrical, galvanic, resistance, and hydrogen probes. Operators should refer to available recommended practices provided by national consensus standards organizations, such as the American Petroleum Institute, the National Association of Corrosion Engineers, and the Gas Piping Technology Committee (GPTC) for guidance in addressing internal corrosion issues.

OPS has worked with GPTC to revise the Guide for Gas Transmission and Distribution Piping Systems (Guide) to better address the control of internal corrosion. GPTC is considering modifying the Guide to address design considerations, corrective measures and detection techniques for internal corrosion.

II. Advisory Bulletin August 29, 2000

To: Owners and Operators of Gas Transmission Pipelines.

Subject: Internal Corrosion in Gas Transmission Pipelines.

Purpose: To advise owners and operators of natural gas transmission pipelines of the need to review their internal corrosion monitoring programs and operations.

Advisory: Owners and operators of natural gas transmission pipelines should review their internal corrosion monitoring programs and consider factors that influence the formation of internal corrosion, including gas quality and operating parameters. Operators should give special attention to pipeline alignment features that may contribute to internal corrosion by allowing condensates to settle out of the gas stream. This action follows a review of incidents involving internal corrosion, some of which resulted in loss of life, injuries, and significant property damage. OPS' preliminary investigation of a recent gas transmission pipeline incident found internal wall thinning on damaged pipe associated with the incident. The wall thinning is consistent with that caused by internal corrosion.

Gas transmission owners and operators should thoroughly review their internal corrosion management programs and operations:

Review procedures for testing to determine the existence or severity of internal corrosion associated with their pipelines. Some methods for monitoring internal corrosion are weight loss coupons, radiography, water chemistry tests, in-line inspection tools, and electrical, galvanic, resistance and hydrogen probes.

Special attention should be given to specific conditions, including flow characteristics, pipeline location (especially drips, deadlegs, and sags, which are on-line segments that are not cleaned by pigging or other methods, fittings and/or "stabbed" connections which could affect gas flow), operating temperature and pressure, water content, carbon dioxide and hydrogen sulfide content, carbon dioxide partial pressure, presence of oxygen and/or bacteria, and sediment deposits.

Review conditions in pipeline segments downstream of gas production and storage fields.

Review conditions in pipeline segments with low spots, sharp bends, sudden diameter changes, and fittings that restrict flow or velocity. These features can contribute to the formation of internal corrosion by allowing condensates to settle out of the gas stream.

www.ingramcontent.com/pod-product-compliance
Lightning Source LLC
Chambersburg PA
CBHW080904290526
45795CB00007BA/2398